Gamification at Work

Designing Engaging Business Software

JANAKI KUMAR & MARIO HERGER

GAMIFICATION AT WORK

DESIGNING ENGAGING BUSINESS SOFTWARE

TITLE: Gamification at Work: Designing Engaging Business Software

AUTHORS: Janaki Mythily Kumar and Mario Herger

PUBLISHER: The Interaction Design Foundation

EDITION NUMBER: 1

ISBN PAPERBACK EDITION: 978-87-92964-07-6

ISBN ONLINE EDITION: 978-87-92964-06-9

ISBN EBOOK EDITION: 978-87-92964-08-3

ISBN HARDBACK EDITION:

COPY EDITOR: Ailsa Campbell

REFERENCE VALIDATION: Armin Walinsky

GRAPHICS, INTERIOR DESIGN, AND COVER: Roland Szattler and Mads Soegaard

COPYRIGHT CLEARANCE: Michael Thorman

PROOFREADER: Ailsa Campbell

SUPERVISORY EDITORS: Mads Soegaard and Rikke Friis Dam

EDITORIAL ASSISTANT: Soeren Dam

TYPOGRAPHY: This text is set in Georgia

COPYRIGHT: See section on Copyright

PEER REVIEW: This book has undergone double-blinded peer-review based on the reviewing guidelines

FRONT PAGE COVER: Cover design is inspired by - and includes graphical elements visually similar to - the iconic PAC-MAN(TM), which is a trademark and copyright of NAMCO BANDAI Games Inc.

Production and dissemination of this work has been funded in part by SAP.

Table of Contents

Foreword

Gamification is becoming a common buzzword in business these days. In its November 2012 press release[1], Gartner predicted that *"by 2015, 40% of Global 1000 organizations will use gamification as the primary mechanism to transform business operations"*. In the same report, they also predicted that *"by 2014, 80% of current gamified applications will fail to meet business objectives, primarily due to poor design"*.

What is gamification? Does it belong in the workplace? Are there design best practices that can increase the efficacy of enterprise gamification efforts?

Janaki Kumar and Mario Herger answer these questions and more. They caution against taking a "chocolate covered broccoli" approach of simply adding points and badges to business applications and calling them gamified. They outline a methodology called Player Centered Design which is a practical guide for user experience designers, product managers and developers to incorporate the principles of gamification into their business software. **Player Centered Design** involves the following five steps:

1. Know your player
2. Identify the mission

---

1. Gartner November 28th Gamification Trends and Strategies to Help Prepare for the Future. Burke. B. http://www.gartner.com/it/content/2191900/2191918/november_28_gamification_bburke. pdf?userId=61080590

3. Understand human motivation
4. Apply mechanics
5. Manage, monitor and measure

Kumar and Herger provide examples of enterprise gamification, introduce legal and ethical considerations, and provide pointers to other resources to continue your journey in designing gamification that works.

Preface

This book is for practitioners by practitioners. Our objective is to share our experiences and stimulate a dialog on this emerging topic. This book does not prescribe recipes for gamification since the best practices are still emerging. Instead it provides a framework to structure gamification projects, which we call Player Centered Design, along with a curated set of resources to help guide practitioners along the journey.

Throughout the book, we share a case study of the SAP Community Network (SCN). We share insights from this project to illustrate points made in each chapter. We provide additional case studies in the Enterprise Gamification Examples chapter.

Enterprise gamification is still in its infancy. There is much more to pursue and learn. In this book, we present what we have learned thus far, to help practitioners on their journey towards mastery of gamification at work.

Introduction

This book covers the intersection of enterprise software and gamification.

Enterprise software refers to software that businesses use to run their day-to-day activities such as finance, sales, human resources, manufacturing, shipping, and procurement. It is typically purchased by companies as off-the-shelf software, customized and configured to meet their business needs, and made available to their employees. Enterprise software provides visibility to executives regarding the health of their organizations and enables them to make course corrections as needed.

Gamification is the application of game design principles and mechanics to non-game environments. It attempts to make technology more inviting by encouraging users to engage in desired behaviors and by showing the path to mastery. From a business viewpoint, gamification is using people's innate enjoyment of play.

Gamification is a buzzword in business these days. Both *Fortune Magazine*[2] and *Wall Street Journal*[3] noted this trend in 2011. M2 Research predicts that the gamification market will reach 2.8 billion dollars by 2016[4].

---

2. Gartner November 28th Gamification Trends and Strategies to Help Prepare for the Future. Burke. B. http://www.gartner.com/it/content/2191900/2191918/november_28_gamification_bburke. pdf?userId=61080590

3. http://blogs.wsj.com/tech-europe/2011/05/04/gamification-hype-or-game-changer/

4. M2 Research Fall 2011: http://www.m2research.com/

There are many reasons for this trend: the changing nature of information work, entry into the workforce of digital natives[5] - a new generation that has grown up playing online and video games, and the wide spread adoption of social media and mobile technology. Businesses are turning to gamification both to engage their customers and to motivate their employees.

As with any innovative trend, best practices in gamification are still emerging. Some businesses are taking a "chocolate covered broccoli" approach, simply adding game mechanics such as points, badges and leaderboards to their applications and calling them "gamified."

Gartner, in a 2012 press release, predicts, that while gamification has enormous potential, by 2014, 80% of current gamified applications will fail to meet business objectives, primarily due to poor design"[6].

"Most attempts at gamification currently miss the mark due to poor design, but successful and sustainable gamification can convert customers into fans, turn work into fun, or make learning a joy. The potential is enormous."

Brian Burke, research vice president at Gartner

This book explores the application of design best practices to gamification to increase the chance of success of gamification. It outlines a process called **Player Centered Design**, which offers a five-step approach to gamification that works.

This book is designed to be a practical guide for user experience professionals, product managers and developers who wish to incorporate the principles of gamification into their business software to make it more engaging to their target audience.

Chapter 1 prepares you to evangelize gamification in your organization, and set the right expectations to achieve success.

---

5. http://en.wikipedia.org/wiki/Digital_native

6. http://en.wikipedia.org/wiki/Digital_native

▶ Chapter 2 introduces the concept of **Player Centered Design**. It points out the primary differences between User Centered Design and Player Centered Design, and describes a process that will help structure your gamification endeavors.

▶ Chapter 3 outlines the components of a rich multifaceted **Player** persona.

▶ Chapter 4 describes the **Mission**. We explore various ways to analyze current user behavior, identify the targeted business outcome, and set a S.M.A.R.T mission. We believe it is important to identify the desired goal of your gamification project, before adding game mechanics to your application.

▶ Chapter 5 examines the psychology behind human **Motivation**. We present a curated list of motivational drivers in this chapter.

▶ Chapter 6 delves into the details of **Game Mechanics.** We present a curated list of game mechanics that are relevant to the enterprise.

▶ Chapter 7 tackles the **Managing, Monitoring, and Measuring** gamification. Gamification in an enterprise is a program and not a project. We recommend starting small, monitoring closely, then revising and iterating for optimal business results.

▶ Chapter 8 introduces the **Legal and Ethical considerations** in gamification.

▶ Chapter 9 provides a collection of **Enterprise gamification examples** and links to a website for further examples.

▶ Chapter 10 is about **Leveling Up**. We point you toward a collection of books, experts, and online resources that can guide you further towards gamification mastery.

Throughout the book we use a case study of the SAP Community Network (SCN), which illustrates the points made in the chapter along with lessons learnt.

Thank you for embarking on this journey of gamification with us. We wish you an engaging and rewarding trip.

CHAPTER
1

Mixing Work and Play

"The opposite of play is not work, it is depression"

— *Brian Sutton-Smith*

Humans have an innate enjoyment of play, and games have been part of human civilization since the very beginning. Gamification attempts to incorporate game elements into non-game environments. In this book, we examine the application of these elements into business software, with the goal to enable customers, partners, and employees to interact with the processes and systems of the organization in an engaging fashion.

1.1 BUSTING THE MYTHS

If you are planning to champion gamification in your business software company, we recommend that you prepare for the skeptics. Gamification is a new concept, and is still emerging. Therefore, it is not surprising that people have misconceptions. We present some data about gaming, gamification, and the changing nature of business software that will help you challenge these myths and misconceptions.

1.1.1 *Myth #1: Gamers are all teenagers and enterprise software is for grown-ups*

The most common misunderstanding is that only teenagers are interested in gaming and gamification, and therefore its application is not appropriate to enterprise software.

According to the Entertainment Software Association's[7] 2012 data, the average gamer is 30 years old and has been playing for 12 years. Sixty eight percent of gamers are 18 years of age or older. Not only are gamers not all teenagers, teenagers now are a minority of all gamers.

The demographics of the enterprise worker are changing as well. The so-called *digital natives*[8] have entered the workplace. According to Wikipedia, a *digital native* is a person who was born after 1960, during or after the general introduction of digital technologies and who, through interacting with digital technology from an early age, has a greater understanding of its concepts. They have grown up with access to highly engaging video games and consumer software, and have similar expectations of enterprise software.

1.1.2 *Myth #2: Gamers are all male and businesses have both men and women working for them*

According to the 2012 industry facts from the Entertainment Software Association, forty-seven percent of all players are women, and women over 18 years of age are one of the industry's fastest growing demographics. One of the reasons for this mis-

---

7. The Entertainment Software Association

8. http://en.wikipedia.org/wiki/Digital_native

conception is that people narrowly associate all games with first person, shooter games. However, thirty-three percent of gamers play social games and many play educational games. Women are the majority of "casual game" players on sites like Zynga, Pogo etc[9]. The prevalence of mobile technology, social media and the broadening spectrum of games has invited new gamers, including women, into the fold.

1.1.3 *Myth #3: Gamers are slackers and businesses need their employees motivated to achieve success*

In Jane McGonigal's book *Reality is Broken*[10], and her TED talk *Gaming Can Make a Better World*[11], she shows that gamers are highly motivated individuals who are ready to change the world. *World of Warcraft*, often referred to as WoW, is a massive multiplayer online role-playing game. An average *World of Warcraft* (WoW) player spends 22 hours a week playing this game of strategy and problem solving. The WoW Wiki is second only to Wikipedia in size and content. McGonigal makes the case that this energy and creativity needs to be harnessed and used to solve real world problems.

"My goal for the next decade is to try to make it as easy to save the world in real life as it is to save the world in online games." Jane McGonigal

Scientists at the University of Washington did just that. For over a decade, a team of highly qualified scientists worked on a technique called protein folding as part of a research effort to understand, prevent and treat diseases like HIV/AIDS, cancer and Alzheimer's. They had not made as much progress as they wanted to, and decided to try incorporating gamification. They created a puzzle that allowed

---

9. Social Network Games 2012 Casual Games Sector Report http://www.superdataresearch.com/wp-content/uploads/2011/12/CasualConnectSocialGames2012.pdf

10. Reality Is Broken: Why Games Make Us Better and How They Can Change the World

11. Jane McGonigal: Gaming can make a better word TED talk http://www.ted.com/talks/jane_mcgonigal_gaming_can_make_a_better_world.html and Jane McGonigal: The game that can give you 10 extra years of life < http://www.ted.com/talks/jane_mcgonigal_the_game_that_can_give_you_10_extra_years_of_life.html>

gamers to fold proteins called Foldit[12] and invited the public to play the game online. 47,000 people volunteered for this challenge and solved the problem in 10 days! If presenting the challenge in the form of a well-designed game could unleash the power of creative problem solving by volunteers towards scientific research, imagine what this technique could do for your organization!

1.1.4 *Myth #4: Work and Play do not mix*

Those who present this argument believe that work and play are opposite of one another. However, as Brian Sutton-Smith says, the opposite of play is not work, but depression. People like to work and people like to play, and the goal of a well-designed enterprise gamification system is to make work more engaging, and not distract them from it. This book offers guidance on how to create such a well-designed gamification system.

1.2 YOU HAVE ALREADY BEEN GAMIFIED!

If the above data do not convince the skeptics, you can point out to them that they have already been gamified! Here are common applications of gamification techniques that most people have encountered:

1.2.1 *Frequent flyer programs*

Most people have played the frequent flyer loyalty game that major airlines and hotels offer. These companies incentivize and guide the behavior of their customers — namely to choose their airlines or book rooms in their hotels. Over the years, they have added more aspects to the game through co-branded credit and debit cards. The more you play, the more you win — and, of course, so does the airline or hotel.

---

12. http://fold.it/portal/

1.2.2 *LinkedIn*

The professional networking website encourages users to provide more professional information using a simple gaming technique: the progress indicator. Most people have encountered this indicator telling them they are 95% complete and what they can do to reach 100%. This is a constant reminder to the user that they have an incomplete profile, but it also informs them as to what they need to do to complete it.

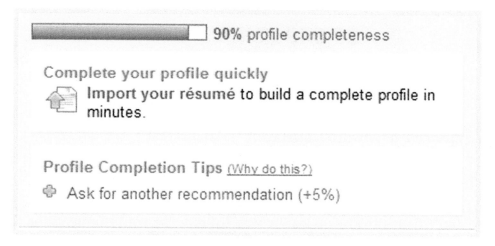

FIGURE 1.1: LinkedIn profile completeness.

Copyright © Linkedin Corporation. All Rights Reserved. Used without permission under the Fair Use Doctrine. See the "Exceptions" section (and subsection "fairUse") of the copyright notice.

Another aspect that LinkedIn uses is the power of community. It shows you simple but powerful network statistics such as how many people are in your network, and how many times your profile has been viewed. You can also see these statistics for others in your network. These are classic uses of game mechanics to encourage you to expand your network and bring more value to LinkedIn.

FIGURE 1.2: LinkedIn network statistics.

Recently, LinkedIn introduced a new way to endorse your connections for their skills. This simple game-like interaction invites you to share your assessment of your connections in your network.

FIGURE 1.3: LinkedIn endorsement requests.

LinkedIn also features a dashboard of endorsements collected for each member. It displays the skills in order of endorsements received, with a thumbnail image of the connection who provided the endorsement.

LinkedIn has designed the Endorsement feature to be simple and fun for the person making the endorsement, and delightful for the person receiving it.

The benefit to LinkedIn is that it brings additional traffic to its site, and enriches the information about their members.

FIGURE 1.4: LinkedIn endorsement statistics .

1.2.3 *Fuel efficient vehicles*

Fuel-efficient cars today encourage driving practices that save energy in multiple ways. They provide real-time feedback on energy consumption on a dashboard as the driver is operating the vehicle. Toyota Prius has such a dashboard that shows the driver if they are using the battery, charging the battery, or using gasoline.

FIGURE 1.5: Prius dashboard.

Copyright © Toyota Motor Corporation . All Rights Reserved. Used without permission under the Fair Use Doctrine. See the "Exceptions" section (and subsection "fairUse") of the copyright notice.

Additionally, some cars such as the Nissan Leaf offer an owners' website that aggregates consumption statistics across a community of drivers.

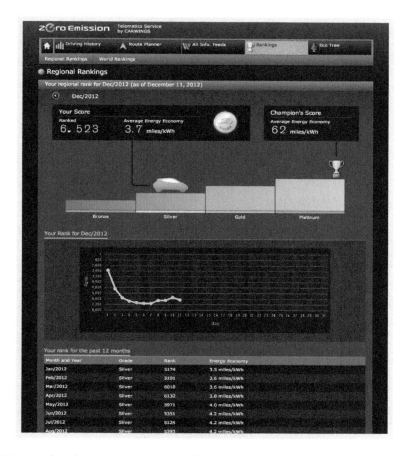

FIGURE 1.6: Nissan leaf owner's personal website.

1.2.4 *Amazon customer reviews*

Community reviews are one of the most successful and pervasive ways to engage customers. Amazon provides a fun way for customers to share their review of the product they have purchased and assign "Stars" based on satisfaction. In its element, assigning ratings and engaging the community are game mechanics in action. Furthermore, reviews themselves can be reviewed! Users can indicate how useful a review was. This in turn enhances a reviewer's reputation on Amazon.

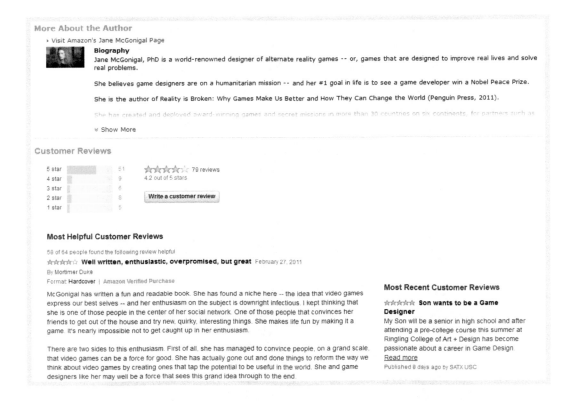

FIGURE 1.7: Amazon community rating system.

1.2.5 *Nike +*

There are many health related gadgets and applications available in the market that use the power of gamification to encourage healthy habits. There are many gamification features in Nike+. You can earn fuel with your Nike FuelBand, and Nike+ Kinect game lets you compete with your friends.

FIGURE 1.8: Nike + Challenge iPhone app.

1.3 CURB OVER-ENTHUSIASM

Unrealistically high expectations of results and under estimation of effort can be just as dangerous for your gamification efforts as skepticism.

1.3.1 *Gamification is not the same as game design*

Gamification is not necessarily making your business application look like a game. Simple game mechanics (like the LinkedIn progress bar) with a clear mission are more powerful than one that lacks a clear purpose and yet has all the bells and whistles such as flashy graphics, visually immersive environments and even sound effects.

1.3.2 *Gamification is not easy*

Gamification is not about slapping on a few points, badges and leaderboards onto your user interface, and concluding that your application has been gamified. Sometimes, a poor attempt at gamification can alienate your users. Gamification is about thoughtful introduction of gamification techniques that engage your users.

1.3.3 *Do no evil*

Gamification is not about manipulating your users, but about motivating them. Ultimately, it is about good design — and good design treats the user with respect. We briefly discuss the ethical considerations of gamification in Chapter 8.

1.3.4 *Gamification cannot fix a bad business model*

Adding badges and points to an ill-conceived business concept will not magically make it viable. However, a well thought out business mission can benefit from a careful application of game mechanics in accelerating adoption and engaging its employees, customers and community.

1.4 WE CAN LEARN A LOT FROM GAMES

Imagine your favorite game and think about why it was so enjoyable and engaging. Now imagine your work life. Would it be so bad, if your work felt a little bit like your favorite game?

Here is a comparison of the attributes of game and work.

	Game	Work
Tasks	repetitive, but fun	repetitive and dull
Feedback	constantly	once a year
Goals	clear	contradictory, vague
Path to Mastery	clear	unclear
Rules	clear, transparent	unclear, nontransparent
Information	right amount at the right time	not the right amount and delivered at the wrong time
Failure	expected, encouraged, spectacular, brag about it	forbidden, punished, don't talk about it
Status of Users	transparent, timely	hidden
Promotion	meritocracy	kiss-up-o-cracy
Collaboration	yes	maybe
Speed/Risk	high	low
Autonomy	high	mid to low
Narrative	yes	only if you are lucky
Obstacles	intentional	accidental

TABLE 1.1: Comparison of the attributes of game and work.

It is clear that we have a lot to learn from game design to make work more engaging and enjoyable.

1.5 SUMMARY

Gamification is a new concept in the context of enterprise software. As with any emerging trend, there are many misconceptions regarding gamification. In this chapter, we have summarized the key myths, and "busted" them with data and real world examples. There are several examples of gamification in consumer software today designed to motivate and engage the user. Finally, it is important to manage your own unrealistic expectations as well as that of stakeholders, to ensure the sustained success of your gamification endeavors.

1.6 INSIGHTS FROM SAP COMMUNITY NETWORK

In 2003, SAP introduced the SAP Community Network (SCN). When it was launched, it was an untested idea with an uncertain outcome. Now it is a two-million member community of SAP professionals that blog, help each other by sharing their technical expertise, create FAQs on several hundred topics, organize meetings and network at official SAP events. Members connect on a personal level as well. They get together informally, share baby pictures, show their office desk setups including fancy coffee machines, and discuss many other non-work related topics. This is one of the secret ingredients of every successful community: people mix work, private life, and fun to make the community their own.

At the end of each chapter, we will share insights of how SCN was gamified and the resulting impact on the community.

To be continued at the end of next chapter...

YOUR NOTES AND THOUGHTS ON CHAPTER 1

Record your notes and thoughts on this chapter. If you want to share these thoughts with others online, go to the bottom of the page at: http://www.interaction-design.org/books/gamification_at_work/chapter_1_ mixing_work_and_play.html

NOTES:

_____

_____

_____

_____

_____

_____

_____

_____

CHAPTER
2

Player Centered Design

"Games give us unnecessary obstacles that we volunteer to tackle."

— Jane McGonigal

When starting to implement gamification into your enterprise software, it may be difficult to know where to begin. It is tempting to jump straight to mechanics and start thinking about points, badges, and leaderboards. Instead, we suggest a different approach. We recommend a process inspired by a well-established design philosophy called User Centered Design.

2.1 WHAT IS USER CENTERED DESIGN?

User Centered Design is a philosophy that puts the user, and their goals, at the center of the design and development process. It strives to develop products that are tightly aligned with the user's needs.

In contrast, poorly designed products are a result of Data Centered Design, or Technology Centered Design, which considers technical artifacts such as the database tables, to create a series of forms that allows the user to "put and get" the data. Developers are naturally drawn to this approach because it is easy to achieve technically, and is the path of least resistance when the team is under time pressure. Moreover, engineers have a clear mental model of the data, and may assume that everyone shares this. However, it has been proven repeatedly that most users do not share this view of the application. They are busy getting their job done, interacting with others, and having fun.

While User Centered Design is certainly better than Data Centered Design, we believe that introducing gamification into software requires the designer to go one step further and use a process that we call Player Centered Design.

2.2 BEYOND USER CENTERED DESIGN

Designers who adopt the user centered design philosophy in their daily work pay attention to the user's goals, and strive to build products that help the user achieve them in an efficient, effective, and satisfactory manner[13].

While effectiveness, efficiency, and satisfaction are worthy goals, gaming and gamification extends and adds increased engagement to these goals. In the context of a game, players voluntarily seek challenges to enhance their playing experience. They seek empowerment over efficiency, delight and fun over mere satisfaction. These factors increase their level of engagement in the game.

2.3 OVERVIEW OF PLAYER CENTERED DESIGN PROCESS

To help designers deal with these changing rules and rising expectations, we in-

---

13. The International Standards Organization (ISO) defines Usability as "The extent to which a product can be used by specified users to achieve specified goals with effectiveness, efficiency, and satisfaction in a specified context of use."

troduce a concept called Player Centered Design that puts the player at the center of the design and development process. The figure below illustrates the process of Player Centered Design and outlines the various steps to help structure your gamification project.

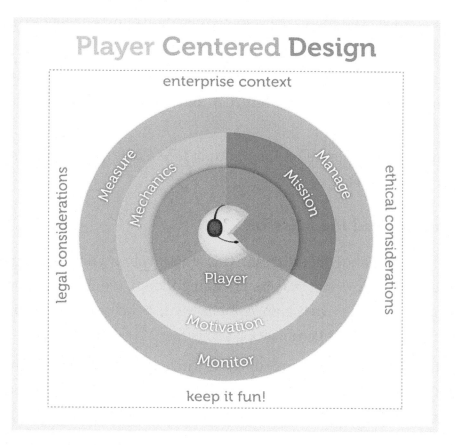

FIGURE 2.1: Player Centered Design Process.

Courtesy of Janaki Kumar and Mario Herger. Copyright: CC-Att-ND (Creative Commons Attribution-NoDerivs 3.0 Unported).

The goal of this process is to provide a framework in which to think about gamification. It is not meant to be a series of rigid, uni-directional steps, but rather an iterative and adaptive framework. We encourage you to review this process in the context of your own organization and modify it if needed, while closely monitoring results.

2.3.1 *Understand the player*

The first step in the player centered design approach is to understand the player and his/her context. The success of your gamification efforts depends on this clear understanding.

Is your player a sales representative, a financial controller, an employee, a supplier, or a customer? Identify him/her and understand as much as you can about him/her.

Chapter 3 will elaborate on the multiple facets of a player and his/her relationship to gaming preferences.

2.3.2 *Understand the Mission*

The next step is to define the Mission. This step involves understanding the current business scenario (what players are doing today), identifying the desired or target business outcome (what management wants to achieve), and setting an appropriate mission for your gamification project.

Chapter 4 outlines the techniques that will help analyze the current scenario and identify the target business outcome. The chapter offers guidelines to set a specific, measurable, actionable, realistic and time-bound (S.M.A.R.T.) gamification mission based on this analysis.

Player centered design is an iterative process. Therefore, while defining the mission, you will learn more about the player; it is worthwhile to consider this new information and its impact on gamification.

2.3.3 *Understand Human Motivation*

There are a number of theories of human motivation. We recommend you familiarize yourself with the latest research on motivation in order to create effective game mechanics. Chapter 5 will present a curated list of motivational drivers to get you started and introduce you to additional resources.

2.3.4 *Apply Game Mechanics*

Armed with a clear understanding of the player, the mission, and the theory behind human motivation, it is time to apply game mechanics, and create a positive flow for your gamification project. Game mechanics refer to the UI elements with which a player interacts such as badges, points, leaderboards and many more. Chapter 6 provides a list of game mechanics relevant to enterprise software.

2.3.5 *Manage, Monitor and Measure*

Gamification is a program and not a project. Therefore, it is important to start small, closely monitor progress, and adjust as needed. The mission needs to be managed, the motivation needs to be monitored, and mechanics need to be measured continuously.

Chapter 7 elaborates on how to manage gamification of enterprise software successfully, and increase player engagement. It offers tips for success in a corporate environment.

2.3.6 *Other considerations in the enterprise context*

Chapter 8 elaborates on the legal and ethical considerations that impact gamification in the context of the enterprise. Privacy and workers' protection practices vary between countries, and what may be legal in one country may not be in another.

The ethics of gamification need to be considered as part of any project. Gamification can be used to engage and motivate, but never manipulate.

The ultimate goal of gamification is to engender positive emotions in the player such as fun, trust and delight. It is important not to forget this when working on the serious aspects of gamification.

We provide a number of enterprise gamification examples in chapter 9, with a link to a website with many more.

2.4 SUMMARY

In this chapter, we have presented a process of gamification, which we call Player Centered Design. It is inspired by User Centered Design, but goes beyond UCD to incorporate the concept of engagement. The process begins with a good understanding of both the player and the mission. This is followed by psychological research on motivation. Based on this solid foundation, we advocate a thoughtful application of game mechanics. We recommend you start small, monitoring closely for best results. The enterprise context including legal and ethical considerations cannot be ignored. And remember to make it fun!

2.5 INSIGHTS FROM SAP COMMUNITY NETWORK

The SCN launch team conducted dozens of interviews with developers inside and outside SAP to understand their work practices, the way they learnt about new technologies, and how they communicated with their personal network.

The interviews revealed a number of interesting facts that later became crucial to the success of this professional community. For example, developers tend to be very open in their communication and are willing to share their expertise. They are less concerned about legal issues, or trade secrets. They prefer to tell the community candidly what is working in the software and what is not. Developers stated that it was important for them to assist their network. They believed that it was more beneficial to do so for their employers than to keep their knowledge to themselves. This information helped us to understand the SCN players, their mission and their motivations.

To be continued at the end of next chapter...

YOUR NOTES AND THOUGHTS ON CHAPTER 2

Record your notes and thoughts on this chapter. If you want to share these thoughts with others online, go to the bottom of the page at: http://www.interaction-design.org/books/gamification_at_work/chapter_2_player_centered_design.html

NOTES:

CHAPTER
3

Player

"In every real man a child is hidden that wants to play."

— Friedrich Nietzsche

3.1 KNOW YOUR PLAYER

Knowing your target audience is important to the success of any design endeavor, and gamification is no exception. It is helpful to know if you are trying to engage a twenty-five-year-old male call center agent or a forty-five-year-old female finance professional. To be successful, just as in user experience design, the gamification strategy needs to be based on a good understanding of your player.

Amy Jo Kim[14], a renowned author and designer of social games, has contributed to popular games such as Rock Band, Sims Online, Moshi Monsters, and many others. She urges game designers to refer to the target audience as players

---

14. http://amyjokim.com/

instead of users, the term used in the software design industry. This distinction highlights the fact that the players' participation is voluntary[15] and they could walk away at any moment. This advice holds true for gamification as well. Gamification does not simply serve a utilitarian purpose, but aims to engage, motivate and delight, which is similar to how a successful game designer approaches its audience.

3.2 USING PERSONAS AS A DESIGN TOOL

The first step in Player Centered Design is to create a rich multi-facetted player persona. This is an enhanced version of a user persona — a fictional archetypal user that is created during the design process. User persona is a design artifact that represents the characteristics, behaviors, and relevant needs of the target user. Persona or user profiles are useful for the following reasons:

▶ They anchor the product team's imagination around the end user. It prevents them from designing for the elastic user, which happens when various features and functions are added on as the project proceeds, resulting in a confusing and sub-optimal end-user product experience.

▶ They guide the team's decision-making and prioritization during the design process.

▶ They create empathy for the end users, and humanize their needs. Personas or profiles remind the team of the ultimate recipient of their hard work.

A typical user persona, in a business software context, describes the user's busi-

---

15. Player participation is voluntary in a game. In business software, however, employees are expected to use the software as part of their work, which is not voluntary. However, we recommend designing the use of gamification aspects of business software to be voluntary while other aspects of the software may not be so.

ness goals, experience and aspirations, along with basic demographic information such as age, gender and education. Enterprise software products tend to target more than one persona due to the interplay of different specializations and roles within a business context. In cases where there are multiple personas interacting with the system, some may be identified as primary, while others may be secondary or supplementary. Fig 3.1 is an example of three user personas in a call center.

FIGURE 3.1: Example User Persona for Customer Service agents.

Courtesy of Janaki Kumar. Copyright: CC-Att-SA (Creative Commons Attribution-ShareAlike 3.0 Unported).

The best way to gather information for your persona is to observe the target users in their natural environment. This technique is called site visits/field research, or contextual inquiry. We have provided a curated list of research techniques in the Appendix section of this book.

3.3 PLAYER PERSONA

When introducing gamification, we recommend that you go beyond the basics to understand the player's personality. This will provide an insight into how to motivate him/her using gamification.

In this chapter, we provide a template that you can use to gather this information. You may use this as a starting point and modify it for your needs.

3.3.1 *Basic demographic information*

Demographics are an important aspect of players' multifaceted personae and provide critical insights on how to engage and motivate them in an enterprise context.

3.3.1.1 Gender

The best way to get this information is to conduct a site visit to a target department(s) that will use the product and observe the distribution of males vs. females. If males form a clear majority, make your persona a male, and if not, make it female. If the distribution is 50/50, the choice is yours. Some product teams may specifically want to target a gender to increase market share. In this case, the persona may be of this targeted gender even if it does not form the majority today.

Why is this relevant to gamification? It provides critical input into the type of game mechanics that will engage the user. Studies have shown that traditional games such as competitive games tend to attract males, while social and mobile games attract females. Having this knowledge upfront can give valuable guidance to the product team with regard to gamification.

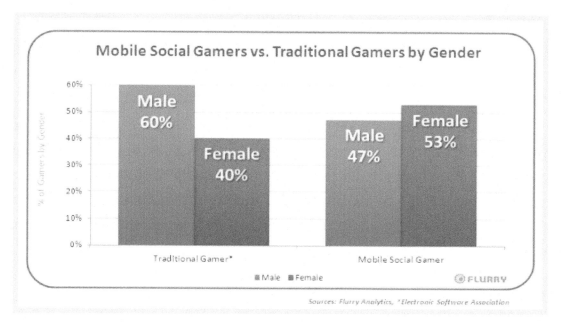

FIGURE 3.2: Distribution of mobile social gamers vs. traditional gamers by gender. Source: Flurry Analytics, Electronics Software Association.

3.3.1.2 Generation

Similar to gender, the best way to get players' generation information is to observe a typical department or group that is using or will use the product. An alternative method is to send out a survey to the target users and gather basic demographic information. Yet another approach is to do research online using LinkedIn or Facebook to understand the generation of the target user.

Research shows that there are significant differences in attitudes between the generations in the way they approach work. Generation X or Gen X refers to those born between the early 1960s and the early 1980s. They tend to be hierarchy oriented and do not tolerate failure.

Generation Y or Gen Y refers to those born from the early 1980s to the early 2000s. This generation grew up with videogames, they expect immediate feedback, and they are willing to take risks and endure "epic failure"[16] . They have 10,000+ hours of experience of video gaming experience under their belts.

This knowledge is relevant for gamification since it gives a good indication of the receptiveness of the player to game mechanics. For example, Gen Y players may have a higher expectation of system feedback than Gen X, and may be more willing to explore the product to learn about its capabilities. These are important clues to which you should pay attention when gamifying your product or service.

3.3.2 *Professional information*

The context of the enterprise and the players' professional information consists of the following aspects:

3.3.2.1 **Type of business or industry**

In the enterprise software context, Industry refers to the category of the business at which the software is targeted. Examples of industries are healthcare, retail, high-tech, finance, consumer-products and education. This is an important aspect of the player persona and gamification. Each industry has unique norms and practices and these need to be considered as part of defining an effective gamification strategy.

To identify the target industry, a good place to start is to interview vision keepers or key stakeholders. Other good techniques for early concept stages are surveys or questionnaires, focus groups, observation, co-innovation partnerships with strategic customers, analyst reports. For new releases of existing products,

---

16. Epic Fail -"A mistake of such monumental proportions that it requires its own term in order to successfully point out the unfathomable shortcomings of an individual or group", http://www.urbandictionary.com

good sources of information are customer lists and web analytics, specifically usage data (if available).

Even when creating a standard product offering that will fit a variety of industries, it is good practice to document the product team's assumptions with regard to target industries to create transparency and a common vision.

3.3.2.2 Job title or job role

The job title or role is an important part of a person's professional identity, both internal and external to the organization. Examples of job titles are software developer, sales representative, assembly line supervisor, call center manager. Examples of roles are customer, supplier, teacher, student, doctor, nurse, and citizen.

It is important to capture this as part of the player persona since it will provide valuable ideas for future design possibilities such as the type of badges and levels that will appeal to this player.

How to get this information: If this is a new product, techniques such as interviews, online research via professional communities like LinkedIn, market research documents could be a good place to start. If this is an incremental release, an online survey targeted at existing users can yield interesting insights into job title norms in your user community.

3.3.2.3 Job goals

To truly understand the nature of the job, it is not sufficient to simply note the job title; you need to look into the details of the job goals. A sales representative in one company may have different responsibilities from a sales representative in another depending on the industry, size of the company and experience of the individual. This information can provide valuable insights when it comes to gamification.

How to get this information: For version one products, online job sites such as Monster.com and LinkedIn can be a good place to start the research. Conducting 1:1

interviews with target players is a great way to learn the full breadth of the job responsibility.

3.3.2.4 Pain points

Identifying user's pain points can go far to uncover design opportunities. Incorporating these pain points into the player persona can be inspirational to the product team in finding creative solutions to them, or providing incentives to the player via gamification.

Direct observation is one way to identify pain points. This may be combined with a structured interview to allow players to express their pain-points directly. If this is an existing product, web analytics and usage data combined with problems reported by existing users can offer rich insights.

3.3.2.5 Aspirations

Aspirations, in the context of the enterprise, could relate to the players' career aspirations, or wish list for the product. For example, in a customer service context the player may want to be considered a product expert among his peers. Including this as part of the persona humanizes the player and helps the product team gain empathy towards him/her.

The best way to get this information is through qualitative research, such as interviews, or surveys. It may take a skilled researcher to elicit this information from a player. One way is to list potential aspirations, and ask the player to rank them by relevance.

3.3.3 *Work Culture*

Effective enterprise gamification strategy needs to be based on a solid understanding of work culture. Work culture has the following aspects:

3.3.3.1 Formal vs. Informal

A finance department may be more formal than a creative department. A high tech company is more informal than a bank. This information is useful in designing the general tone of gamified software.

3.3.3.2 Competitive vs. Cooperative

Interestingly, competition is not always motivating to all player types. Cooperation and collaboration may be more motivating in some cases. Understanding the player's response to competition provides valuable insight into selecting the appropriate gamification strategy. For example, leaderboards are effective in motivating competitive individuals, and may be demotivating to others.

3.3.3.3 Structured vs. Unstructured

Some work cultures are more structured than others are. While some may provide strict guidance to their employees on their tasks and responsibilities, other environments may hold them responsible for the business outcome, and allow more freedom to the employees on the exact tasks.

3.3.3.4 Individual Achievement vs. Team Achievement

The culture of the player's environment has a big impact on the success of gamification. Does the culture emphasize harmony over competition? Alternatively, does the culture reward individual over group achievement? These are very important aspects to consider when designing game mechanics.

For example, if the culture focuses on harmony, over-emphasis on mechanics that engender individual achievements (such as leaderboards) may not be a good fit. When the design is not a good cultural fit, it may result in demotivation and negative perception of the gamification efforts.

3.3.4 *Player Type*

Richard Bartle has created the Bartle test of Psychology[17] that classifies players into four categories based on their gaming preference. They are Achiever, Explorer, Socializer and Killer.

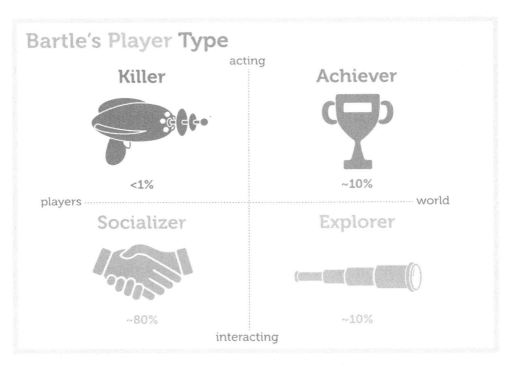

FIGURE 3.3: Bartle Player Types.

Courtesy of Janaki Kumar and Mario Herger. Copyright: CC-Att-ND (Creative Commons Attribution-NoDerivs 3.0 Unported).

Everyone has elements of all four-player types to some degree. The Bartle test determines the dominant distribution.

- ▶ Achievers play to gain points and status. The frequent flier statuses appeal to Achievers. Ten percent of players are of this type.

- ▶ Explorers love to discover new aspects of the game. They do not mind spending time doing repetitive tasks to unlock new levels of

---

17. http://en.wikipedia.org/wiki/Bartle_Test

the game. Discovering "Easter Eggs" &mdash[18]; brings special joy to Explorers. Ten percent of players are of this type.

▶ Socializers play for the joy of interacting with others rather than for the game itself. Facebook games such as Farmville appeal to socializers. The majority of players (as much as 80%) fall into this category.

▶ Killers are similar to Achievers in that they like to win points and status. However, they go one-step further and find joy in seeing others lose. Interestingly, less than 1% of players are of this type.

This test is available to the public at <http://www.gamerdna.com/quizzes/bartle-test-of-gamer-psychology>

Understanding the type of player will help you choose the game mechanics that will be most appealing to your target audience.For example, if you are designing an application for Sales Representatives and you observe that they are mostly Killer and Achiever player types, a prominent display of leaderboard may be motivating to your player. If your players are mostly Socializers, mechanics that enable community collaboration may be more engaging than a leaderboard.

3.4 PLAYER PERSONA TEMPLATE

Here is a template of the player persona for your use. It allows you to represent all aspects of the player persona concisely. You may use this as a starting point and modify it based on your needs.

---

18. Easter eggs, are hidden elements of a computer program: a secret message, graphic, animation, or sound effect hidden in a computer program and activated by a specific undocumented sequence of key-strokes. An Easter egg is typically intended as a harmless joke or as a way to display the credits of the program's development team.

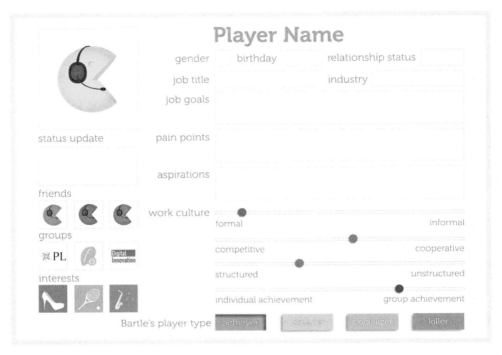

FIGURE 3.4: Player persona template.

Courtesy of Janaki Kumar and Mario Herger. Copyright: CC-Att-ND (Creative Commons Attribution-NoDerivs 3.0 Unported).

3.5 SUMMARY

The first step in successful gamification is to know your player. A player persona is a design artifact that captures the multi-dimensionality of the player including demographics, professional goals, pain-points, aspirations, and work culture and player type. In this chapter, we have provided a template that you can use to create a player persona — an important part of creating an effective gamification strategy for your enterprise application.

3.6 INSIGHTS FROM SAP COMMUNITY NETWORK

With the information gathered through the interviews (referred to in the previous chapter), developer personas started to emerge. They typically are highly paid professionals, who work in IT for an SAP customer or as a consultant. Their success depends on open communication with their peers. They are expected to combine their deep technical expertise with business knowledge to build applications for their business users quickly and effectively.

If they are new in their role, they need to quickly learn the basics and understand the range of technical capabilities that are available. Experienced and highly skilled professionals on the other hand, look for guidance to solve complex problems, and for recommendations on IT strategy. The players are looking for a wide range of information from code snippets, to complete blue prints to implement SAP solutions, to best practices per industry. Furthermore, they are usually under time pressure and need this information quickly.

FIGURE 3.5: SCN Player persona.

Courtesy of Janaki Kumar and Mario Herger. Copyright: CC-Att-ND (Creative Commons Attribution-NoDerivs 3.0 Unported).

To be continued at the end of next chapter...

YOUR NOTES AND THOUGHTS ON CHAPTER 3

Record your notes and thoughts on this chapter. If you want to share these thoughts with others online, go to the bottom of the page at: http://www.interaction-design.org/books/gamification_at_work/chapter_3_player.html

NOTES:

_____

_____

_____

_____

_____

_____

_____

_____

CHAPTER
4

Mission

"Begin with the end in mind"
"Seek first to understand, then to be understood"

— *Stephen Covey*

Mission refers to the goal of your gamification activity. It has to be identified with care, since it determines the ultimate success or failure of your efforts. In this chapter we will discuss the aspects to consider when choosing a meaningful mission that can be used internally by the gamification team to guide their endeavors.

4.1 STEPS TO CREATE AN EFFECTIVE MISSION

The key aspects to consider in setting an effective mission are:

▶ Understand the current scenario

▶ Understand the target business outcome

▶ Identify a S.M.A.R.T. Mission

Begin with a good understanding of the problem you are trying to solve, and the outcome you are trying to achieve; based on this understanding, set a S.M.A.R.T mission.

Let us examine each of these steps in detail.

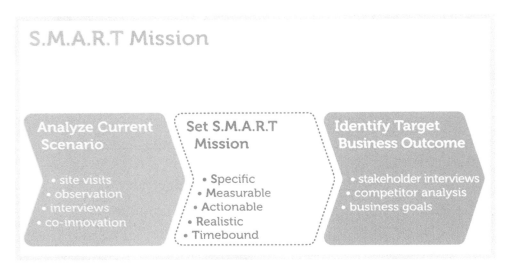

FIGURE 4.1: Analyze current scenario, understand target business outcome and set a S.M.A.R.T. mission.

Courtesy of Janaki Kumar and Mario Herger. Copyright: CC-Att-ND (Creative Commons Attribution-NoDerivs 3.0 Unported).

4.1.1 *Analyze Current Situation*

The current scenario is what the players do today. It involves studying the work practices currently followed by the employee, customer, or partner.

The best way to get this information is through qualitative research such as observation, site-visits and interviews. The goal is to develop a strong empathy with the target players. An effective way to do this is through Design Thinking[19]

---

19. http://dschool.stanford.edu/dgift/

a methodology offered by the design school, Hasso Plattner Institute of Design at Stanford University[20].

If the gamified software is for internal use, it is relatively easy to access the target player. If the gamification is part of standard software, however, the level of customer intimacy required may not be achievable through the normal recruiting processes. To overcome this issue, we recommend establishing Co-Innovation Partnerships with a few key customers. For more information on Co-Innovation Partnerships, refer to Appendix A.12.

4.1.2 *Understand the target business outcome*

On a high level, the target scenario is what the management wants employees, customers or partners to do. For example, they may want sales reps to sell more, customers to buy more. However, this is too high level and we need to go deeper to create an effective mission.

The best way to get this information is to interview stakeholders to understand the behavior change they wish to see in the organization.

4.1.3 *Identify a S.M.A.R.T. mission*

Based on an analysis of the current scenario, and an understanding of the target scenario, we can identify a mission for our gamification project. We recommend that the gamification mission be specific, measurable, actionable, realistic and time-bound. These elements are encapsulated in the acronym S.M.A.R.T.

Let us examine the applications of these dimensions in defining a mission in the following case:

Company A's call center has a low customer satisfaction score. Management have examined the cause of this problem and identified that call center agents are not sufficiently knowledgeable about their new product's features and functions,

---

20. http://dschool.stanford.edu/

and are therefore not able to provide satisfactory answers to customer questions. The company has provided on-line training materials for the agents. However, only 10% of the agents have completed the training. The company decides to try gamification to motivate the agents. What is an appropriate Mission for this enterprise gamification project?

For the above case, we do not recommend you choose "Increase Customer Satisfaction" as your gamification mission. Although it is somewhat specific and measurable, it is not actionable, or time-bound.

Rather, we recommend that you look at the root cause relating to lack of training. A more effective mission is to "Increase completion of training activity to 80% in 3 months". This mission is specific, can be measured, is actionable by players, and time-bound. To know if it is realistic in the given time frame, we need to examine the current scenario and the target scenario.

4.1.4 *Additional guidelines for Mission Selection*

4.1.4.1 **Do not get in the way**

Engagement is an important part of any gamification mission. However, select the part of the application to be gamified with care, and select your mission accordingly. Enterprise software's primary objective is about achieving specific business outcomes. Therefore, ensure that gamification does not get in the way of such critical business processes.

4.1.4.2 **Embrace iteration**

Player centered design is iterative. Therefore, information learned at later stages in the process may shed more light on previous stages. For example, during the course of analyzing the current scenario, understanding target scenarios, and identifying the mission, we may learn more about the player. If this were to happen, we can go back and adjust our player persona based on this new information. Iteration is the key to any innovative endeavor, including gamification.

The mission of gamification could be revisited for new releases of the application to maximize business outcome.

4.2 MISSION EXAMPLES

Here are a few non-enterprise examples to illustrate how to identify a mission:

4.2.1 *Example: Everyday fitness*

- ▶ **Current scenario**: The majority of people take the escalator instead of the stairs
- ▶ **Target scenario**: We want people to take the stairs
- ▶ **Mission**: Encourage majority of subway passengers to take the stairs instead of the escalator in a fun and engaging way.

This is what a team did in the Volkswagen project Piano staircase. Check out the video at: Source: http://www.thefuntheory.com/piano-staircase

FIGURE 4.2: Piano Staircase.

4.2.2 *Example: Driving below speed limit*

▶ **Current scenario**: Drivers drive above speed limit

▶ **Target scenario**: We want drivers to obey the posted speed limit

▶ **Mission**: Get more people to drive at or below the speed limit by making it fun to do.

This is the story of Speed Camera lottery that started as a Volkswagen fun project, and was later implemented in Sweden where it reduced average speed from 35 km to 25 km/hour. Check out the video at http://www.thefuntheory.com/speed-camera-lottery-0

FIGURE 4.3: Camera lottery.

4.2.3 *Enterprise Example: What is in a name?*

▶ **Current scenario**
  The company has grown fast, and the employees no longer know their co-workers' names. They feel they are working with strangers. Employee turnover is trending up

▶ **Target scenario**
  Nurture employee camaraderie and reduce employee turnover

▶ **Mission**
  Help majority of employees learn each other's names in 3 months

Every time an employee logs in, he/she is presented with a co-worker's face and three possible names. The employee identifies the co-worker, and gets to learn a little bit about them.

4.3 SUMMARY

The mission refers to the goal of the gamification activity. Setting a good goal for the gamification project involves understanding the current scenario, and target business outcome, and setting an appropriate mission for your gamification project.

Engagement is an important part of any gamification mission. However, in the enterprise context, ensure that gamification does not get in the way of a person's core job. Select a S.M.A.R.T. mission, to allow the team to measure the success of their gamification strategy against this agreed-upon mission.

4.4 INSIGHTS FROM SAP COMMUNITY NETWORK

Having created a player persona, the next step was to identify the mission.

► Current Situation: Complex environment with little support

► SAP's Target Business Outcome: Increase customer satisfaction by increasing the quality of SAP implementations

► Mission of SCN: Help SCN professionals succeed by providing them access to a large community of experts by increasing number of active users, and recognizing excellence by highlighting top contributors

The original assumption was that the most frequent participants in the community would be consultants and IT professionals from large companies. However, it turned out that a large number of early contributors were independent consultants or members of smaller IT teams. They welcomed the connection to other developers. They participated actively in the community and shared their expertise generously. This created a positive momentum, and made visible the helpful and generous spirit of the community. Soon, this encouraged employees from larger companies to engage with a similar community spirit, and they started sharing their knowledge for the benefit of everyone.

The mission of SCN, to share information, learn, and connect with others, was appealing to SAP professionals who did not have a large network of their own. They saw this as an opportunity to become visible to a wider audience.

To be continued at the end of next chapter...

YOUR NOTES AND THOUGHTS ON CHAPTER 4

Record your notes and thoughts on this chapter. If you want to share these thoughts with others online, go to the bottom of the page at: http://www.interaction-design.org/books/gamification_at_work/chapter_4_mission.html

NOTES:

_____

_____

_____

_____

_____

_____

_____

CHAPTER
5

Motivation

"Gamification is 75% Psychology and 25% Technology."

— *Gabe Zichermann*

Understanding human motivation is an important aspect of Gamification. This chapter will provide a sampling of motivational concepts relevant to gamification

5.1 THE PLATINUM RULE

You may have heard of the Golden Rule that says, "Do unto others as you want done unto you". Based on this rule, you assume that you motivate others the way you want to be motivated. We offer a different approach. In the case of Gamification, we prefer the Platinum Rule that states that "Do unto others what they want done unto them". While there are general ways to motivate and demotivate people, the technique that will be most effective will vary based on the Player Profile. Factors such as generation, gender, and goals play a role in determining the right motivation for your player. For example, the most effective motivational technique will vary between a player who is an eighteen-year-old male, where your mission is to help him master a math concept, and a player who is a forty-year-old female accounting professional, where your mission is to motivate her to complete her bank reconciliation by the end of the week. In other words, understand your player, know your mission and think carefully about which motivational technique will help your player achieve the mission.

5.2 INTRINSIC AND EXTRINSIC MOTIVATION

There are two general types of motivation: intrinsic and extrinsic. Intrinsic motivation refers to internal motivations such as autonomy, mastery and meaning. Extrinsic refers to external motivational techniques such as money, trophies etc.

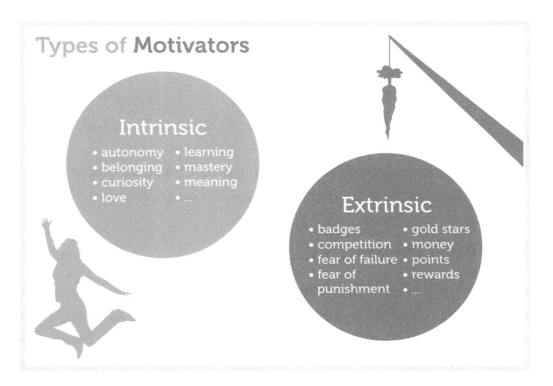

FIGURE 5.1: Intrinsic and extrinsic motivation.

Courtesy of Janaki Kumar and Mario Herger. Copyright: CC-Att-ND (Creative Commons Attribution-NoDerivs 3.0 Unported).

Daniel Pink[21], the author of *Drive*, conducted research at MIT and found that extrinsic motivational techniques are effective for simple, rote tasks. However, when the task requires higher cognitive functions or innovations, extrinsic factors are no longer effective. In fact, they may be de-motivators. Therefore, for complex problem-solving tasks, people are motivated by a sense of **autonomy, mastery, and meaning**. This is an important factor to keep in mind when introducing gamification into the enterprise.

5.3 MORE RESEARCH ON MOTIVATION

Here are pointers to more research on motivation that could be helpful to you in your gamification endeavors:

5.3.1 *Four types of fun*

Fun is an important part of gamification and it is interesting to study the existing research on it. Nicole Lazzaro, founder of XEODesign, categorizes fun into four types:

- ▶ Hard fun which provides the opportunity for challenge, mastery and feelings of accomplishment
- ▶ Easy fun inspired by exploration and role play
- ▶ Serious fun refers to purposeful play and changes how players think, feel, behave and make a difference in the real world
- ▶ People fun provides an excuse to hang out with friends

Nicole presents her research on Fun in this insightful info graphic: http://nicole-lazzaro.com/wp-content/uploads/2012/03/4_keys_poster3.jpg

5.3.2 *B.J. Fogg's Behavior Model*

B.J. Fogg presents his Psychology of Persuasion at http://www.behaviormodel.org/.

---

21. Pink, Daniel. 2009. Drive - The Surprising Truth About What Motivates Us.

He presents a model called the Fogg Behavior model that states that for a certain behavior to happen, you need Trigger, Ability and Motivation. For example, if you need your employee, customer or partner to do something, you need to ensure that all three factors are addressed. They need to receive a trigger (notification or alert with a call to action), they must have the ability to take this action (resources and time), and finally, they must be motivated to take action. He further states that to troubleshoot a lack of action, first address the trigger and ability before trying to address the motivation.

For example, if you want your employees to donate a million dollars to a company's pledge drive, and the donations are not where you want them to be, first check if they received the information about the campaign (via an email, for example), then address the ability (is the donations website working? Does it have a fast response time? Does it take too steps to complete? Are we asking for too much? Try asking for a reasonable amount $10 — $20 in addition to the overall goal of a million). Once you have addressed the trigger and ability, and if you still do not see results, you can motivate them to donate by explaining the importance of the cause and the benefit it will bring. All too often, people tend to believe that their employees do not care for the cause (lack of motivation), when they may not have received the email in the first place (trigger).

5.4   CURATED LIST OF MOTIVATIONAL DRIVERS

Motivational drivers, discussed below, have applicability beyond digital technology. They are based on observations on what motivates people in the real world, and drawing from this knowledge to design engaging experiences in the virtual world.

Here is a curated list of behaviors that drive motivation. This is not meant to be an exhaustive list, but rather a good start to leverage existing research on our natural psychological tendencies to create engaging gamified experiences.

5.4.1 *Collecting*

We enjoy collecting — trading cards, coins, stamps, antique wristwatches, cars or friends on Facebook. Some collections may have monetary value, e.g. trading cards, while other collections may be symbolic of social status, e.g. friends on Facebook. Once we get started on a collection that comes in a "set", we have the urge for "Set Completion". If the set is infinite, we are motivated to keep collecting for the joy it brings us. In some cases, we may compare our collections to others and feel the urge to compete.

5.4.2 *Connecting*

We long to be part of something larger than ourselves. This could mean connecting to other people to be part of a community, or connecting to a cause to be part of something larger and meaningful. We join clubs of various sorts to connect with people like us and have meaningful shared experiences. It validates our existence and makes life more enjoyable.

FIGURE 5.2: Connecting using social media.

Courtesy of WebTreatsETC. Copyright: CC-Att-SA (Creative Commons Attribution-ShareAlike 3.0 Unported).

5.4.3 *Achievement*

We get great satisfaction from achievement, no matter what our Bartle player profile[22]. If we are challenged, we are, more likely than not, motivated to try hard to achieve success. When we do, we get a positive psychological feedback that makes us want to do it again. There are some subtle factors to pay attention to. If the challenge is too difficult or too easy, we may not be as motivated by achievement as we would be if the challenge were just the right level of difficulty.

We do not expect to win every time. A variable schedule of achievement or a chance to win may be enough of a motivator to make us try. Lottery players play for the chance to win even if they know intellectually that the odds of winning are not high.

5.4.4 *Feedback*

We like to receive feedback. This could be as simple as the small nods we get when we talk to people. It communicates, "I heard you. I am paying attention. What you are saying is worth listening to". It motivates us to continue talking to this person. A digital example is Amazon sending us an instant confirmation email when we place an order. It communicates, "We received your order. It is safe with us". It enhances our sense of security and wellbeing.

Not receiving any feedback can be extremely demotivating. If you are talking to someone and they remain impassive, you eventually stop talking, since you are not sure if the other person is listening to you or understands you. Software that gives you no feedback when you perform an action is significantly less enjoyable to use than one that does.

5.4.5 *Self-Expression*

We are entering an era of hyper-personalization enabled by technology. Compa-

---

22. Killer, Achiever, Socializer, Explorer
   http://en.wikipedia.org/wiki/Bartle_Test

nies like Nike are offering customers the ability to specify the exact sizes, features, colors, and styles of their shoes[23]. Players of online games spend time customizing their avatars, from eye and skin color and body shape to accessories like earrings, hats and gloves, to control how they are viewed by other players.

5.4.6 *Reciprocity*

Many of us have had the experience of walking into a store, accepting a "free" sample, and feeling compelled to make a purchase out of a sense of reciprocity. Organizations such as the March of Dimes, Cystic Fibrosis Foundation, World Wildlife Fund, Easter Seals and the American Diabetes Foundation send free address labels to potential donors to leverage this motivational driver as a fund raising technique.

5.4.7 *Blissful Productivity*

Mihaly Csikszentmihalyi (pronounced MEE-hy CHEEK-sent-me-hi-ee), a distinguished professor of Psychology and Management at Claremont Graduate University, is the director of Quality of Life Research Center and has done pioneering work researching human strengths such as optimism, motivation and responsibility. He defined the concept of *Flow* as "The mental state of operating in which a person in an activity is fully immersed in the feeling of energized focus, full involvement and the success in the process of the activity". When a task is too difficult, it causes people to be anxious. When a task is too easy, it causes boredom. When the task is just right, we are in a state of heightened focus and immersion, or in other words a state of *Flow*[24].

---

23. Nike plans to use 3D printing technology to allow consumers to specify their shoes

24. Mihaly Csikszentmihalyi: Flow: The Psychology of Optimal Experience, 1991 Beyond Boredom and Anxiety: Experiencing Flow in Work and Play, 1975

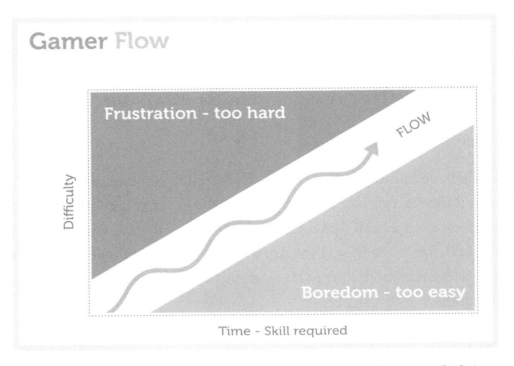

FIGURE 5.3: The concept of Flow introduced by Mihaly Csikszentmihalyi.

Courtesy of Janaki Kumar and Mario Herger. Copyright: CC-Att-ND (Creative Commons Attribution-NoDerivs 3.0 Unported).

Video game players experience this sense of flow when the game is the right level of difficulty for their skill. Games offer levels so users can graduate to increasing difficulty levels as their skills improve. Business software can benefit from incorporating the concept of levels to enable their users to achieve this sense of flow.

5.5 SUMMARY

Understanding human motivation is an important part of creating an effective gamification strategy. Students of gamification could benefit from studying the existing research on motivation. In this chapter, we have curated a list of motivational drivers that we believe are a good place to start. They are collecting, connecting, achievement, feedback, reciprocity, and blissful productivity.

5.6 INSIGHTS FROM SAP COMMUNITY NETWORK

In their 2006 book *The Geek Gap* Bill Pfleging and Melinda Zetlin describe clearly what motivates developers as compared to business people. Developers' motives include learning and mastery, curiosity about new technologies, respect and loyalty towards peers, and generally a playful disposition. They need to stay current with technological trends, or risk becoming obsolete. These trends can include niche technologies that could be used productively in business applications. They value peer recognition over monetary rewards.

The above research was validated by the typical SCN users' behavior. They shared their lessons from projects, they prepared step-by-step guides for the community assembled FAQs, evaluated new technologies, and responded to questions with incredible speed.

The motivational drivers that apply to SCN are connecting with other developers, showcasing their expertise via self-expression, and achieving peer recognition.

To be continued at the end of next chapter

YOUR NOTES AND THOUGHTS ON CHAPTER 5

Record your notes and thoughts on this chapter. If you want to share these thoughts with others online, go to the bottom of the page at: http://www.interaction-design.org/books/gamification_at_work/chapter_5_motivation.html

NOTES:

_____

_____

_____

_____

_____

_____

_____

_____

CHAPTER
6

Mechanics

Game Mechanics are constructs of rules and feedback loops intended to produce enjoyable gameplay. They are the building blocks that can be applied and combined to gamify any non-game context."

— *The Gamification WIKI*

Mechanics are the most visible part of gamification and tend to be the primary focus of most gamification projects. We like to think of game mechanics as paints in an artist's palette. We cannot create great art just by adding many colors to our picture, unless we also have an artistic vision, talent, and training to begin with. Similarly, successful application of game mechanics depends on a well-designed gamification strategy built on a good understanding of the player, the mission, and human motivation.

In this chapter, we present a curated list of game mechanics that may be used as building blocks and combined in strategic ways to achieve the positive engagement loop in your application.

6.1 CURATED LIST OF GAME MECHANICS

FIGURE **6.1**: The Tag cloud of game mechanics.

Courtesy of Janaki Kumar and Mario Herger. Copyright: CC-Att-ND (Creative Commons Attribution-NoDerivs 3.0 Unported).

There are a few collections of game mechanics available online[25]. We find these lists are at different levels of granularity and not all of them are pertinent to enterprise gamification. Therefore, we have curated a list of game mechanics that can help business software designers embark on their gamification journey.

When used appropriately, game mechanics can leverage a natural motivational driver in the player. For example, the motivation driver for collection may be addressed with badges, and the achievement motivation may be addressed by leaderboard. However, in a holistic gamification design, many motivational drivers may be at play. For example, FourSquare players may be motivated by collecting points and badges, achieving the status of mayor in their favorite establishment

25. The Techcrunch scavenger list
        http://techcrunch.com/2010/08/25/scvngr-game-mechanics/,
     and Gamification.org WIKI
        http://gamification.org/wiki/Game_Mechanics#Usage

and connecting with their network while doing so. We will point out the primary motivational driver addressed by each of the game mechanics discussed below.

6.1.1 *Points*

Points are the granular units of measurement in gamification. They are single count metrics. This is the way the system keeps count of the player's actions pertaining to the targeted behaviors in the overall gamification strategy. For example, FourSquare counts each check in, and LinkedIn counts each connection.

Points provide instant feedback to the player, and thus address the feedback motivational driver. Players may also motivated by collection, to see their points count go up.

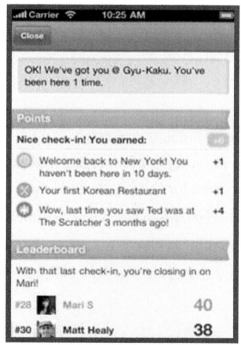

FIGURE 6.2: Foursquare gives points for each check-in.

FIGURE 6.3: LinkedIn counts each connection.

6.1.2 *Badges*

Once the players have accumulated a certain number of points, they may be awarded badges. Badges are a form of virtual achievement by the player. They provide positive reinforcement for the targeted behavior.

Foursquare awards badges when the player has accumulated enough check-ins. Another example of a badge is eBay's top seller virtual "ribbon".

Badges address the motivational driver of collection and achievement.

FIGURE 6.4: Foursquare awards badges.

FIGURE 6.5: eBay awards a top seller virtual ribbon.

6.1.3 *Leaderboards*

Leaderboards bring in the social aspect of points and badges, by displaying the players on a list, typically ranked in descending order with the greatest number of points at the top. The possible disadvantage of a leaderboard is that it could be demotivating to a new player. For example, if player A has 10,000 points, and is on top of the leaderboard, and a new player B has 10 points and is at the bottom, it is likely that player B may become demotivated and give up playing the game. She, or he, may believe that he/she is never going to compete with player A, and therefore why should he/she even try?

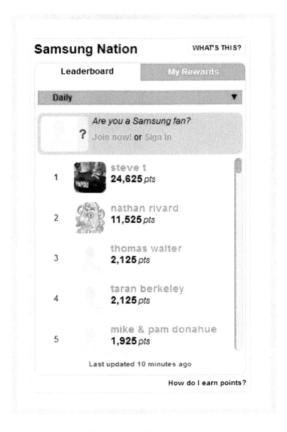

FIGURE 6.6: Samsung Nation leaderboard.

Foursquare has a leaderboard modified into a **cross-situational leader board**. This variant places the logged-in player (Matt Healy in Figure 6.7) in the center and shows similar scoring fellow players above (Tristan Walker) and below (Tim Vetter) for context. The ranking (points) is limited to a set of players who are close to the logged-in player. The goal with this variant of leaderboard is to motivate the player to compete with the players closest to him. Note that a cross-situational leaderboard may be different for each player since it is limited to his or her context. It does not convey an overall ranking of all players.

The achievement motivational driver is addressed via a leaderboard.

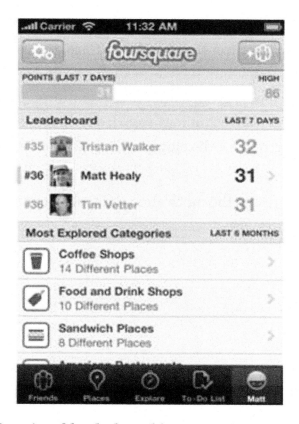

FIGURE 6.7: Cross-situational leaderboard by Foursquare.

6.1.4 *Relationships*

Relationships are game mechanics based on the motivational driver of connection. We are social beings, and relationships have a powerful effect on how we feel and what we do.

Peer pressure is not restricted to school-age children. Adults succumb to it too. In 2010, one of the authors (Janaki Kumar) did research on personal sustainability and one of the findings was that a trusted person in a participant's network had more impact on his or her day-to-day choices than the media. For example, participants were more likely to recycle if a trusted member of their community did so, than if they were told to do so by the media.

Relationships reduce stress in people and are positive motivators. People who are trying to quit bad habits such as alcoholism, or deal with a loss of a loved one have found that support groups offer emotional support and encouragement during a time of need. In the technology world, developer communities are a good example of a support group for developers where they offer and receive technical help.

Relationship addresses the motivational driver of connection.

FIGURE 6.8: Twitter urges me to follow John Maeda and IxDA since people in my current network do so.

6.1.5 *Challenge with epic meaning*

Challenge is a powerful game mechanic to motivate people to action, especially if they believe they are working to achieve something great, something awe-inspiring, and something bigger than themselves.

As we mentioned earlier, scientist at the University of Washington challenged the public to play Foldit[26], a game about protein folding. This game has a scientific purpose behind it. Knowing the structure of the protein in a cell was the key to un-

---

26. Foldit: An online game about protein folding http://fold.it/portal/

derstanding how it works and how to target it with drugs. Since proteins are part of so many diseases, they can also be part of the cure. Folding proteins provides important clues to the scientists on how to prevent or treat diseases such as HIV/AIDS, cancer and Alzheimer's. A team of experts had worked on this problem for over 10 years and had not solved it. Once the scientific challenge was launched in the form of a game, 46,000 volunteer players solved the puzzle in 10 days.

The challenge game mechanic addresses the achievement motivational driver. However, in the case of the Foldit challenge, the feeling of connection and perhaps reciprocity, (if the player had known someone dear to him/her suffering with the illness the challenge was seeking to cure) may have played a part in its overwhelming success.

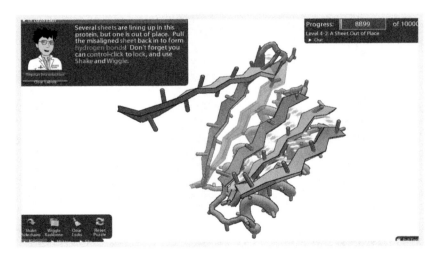

FIGURE 6.9: Foldit, a scientific challenge to citizen scientists that yielded spectacular results.

6.1.6 *Constraints with urgent optimism*

Interestingly, constraints such as deadlines, when combined with urgent optimism, motivate people to action. Urgent Optimism[27] refers to extreme self-motivation. It is the desire to act immediately to tackle an obstacle combined with the belief that we have a reasonable hope of success.

Some registration sites use gamification to reduce the drop off rate by limiting the amount of time the user can take to complete the registration process.

FIGURE 6.10: There are only 11 minutes and 19 seconds to register. Better hurry!.

Copyright © Unknown Author. All Rights Reserved. Used without permission under the Fair Use Doctrine. See the "Exceptions" section (and subsection "fairUse") of the copyright notice.

Gilt, a fashion ecommerce site, constrains the time allowed for their customers to bid on items to motivate them to action.

Players are motivated by achievement when they are faced with these constraints and are driven to overcome them.

---

27. Jane McGonigal in her TED talk presents this idea that in games, a "win or even an "epic win" is possible and therefore worth striving for." http://www.ted.com/talks/jane_mcgonigal_gaming_can_make_a_better_world.html

FIGURE 6.11: This GILT offer Ends Wed 03/24 Midnight EST. Act now!.

6.1.7 *Journey*

The journey game mechanic recognizes that the player is on a personal journey and incorporates this element into the experience. Here are three examples of implementations of this game mechanic:

6.1.7.1 Onboarding

A new player needs to be on boarded since they are just starting the journey. Offering help and a brief introduction to the features and functions motivate the player to embark on the journey.

6.1.7.2 Scaffolding

Scaffolding is a way to help the on boarded, yet inexperienced, user avoid errors and feel a sense of positive accomplishment. A product could progressively disclose more features as the player gains more experience using the product.

6.1.7.3 Progress

Progress refers to providing feedback to the user on where he or she is in the journey, and encouraging him/her to take the next step.

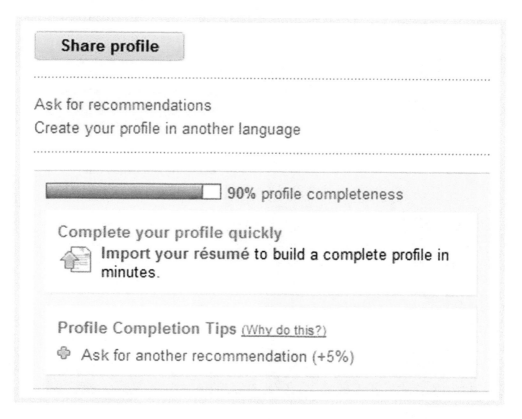

FIGURE 6.12: LinkedIn uses Progress game mechanic to show that the player's profile is 90% complete and offers suggested next steps.

Journey addresses the player's need for blissful productivity, by presenting the right set of features appropriate to the player's level in the game.

6.1.8 *Narrative*

The narrative game mechanic draws the players into a story within the game. Zombie Run, a fitness game, uses narrative to make the players believe that zombies are after them, and they need to run as fast as they can to get away. The object of the game is to motivate the players to get fit without making it explicit.

FIGURE 6.13: Zombies are after you. Run!.

Copyright © Six to Start . All Rights Reserved. Used without permission under the Fair Use Doctrine. See the "Exceptions" section (and subsection "fairUse") of the copyright notice.

Narrative offers the players a chance to express themselves via role-play. In the case of Zombie run, players are motivated by achievement by out-running the zombies.

6.1.9 *Emotion*

As Don Norman eloquently argues in his book *Emotional Design*[28], our emotions do play a role in how we experience a product.

In many ways, emotional design is a large category in and of itself. In the context of gamification, we are not attempting to cover the topic as a whole. Rather, we want to draw inspiration from it, to enrich our gamification designs.

Game designers have led the way in investing in high quality artwork in their products that appeal to our emotions. Consumer products (iPhones, iPads) and websites (Pinterest) are following this trend. Employees experience emotional delight in the consumer software they use, and have similar expectations with enterprise software.

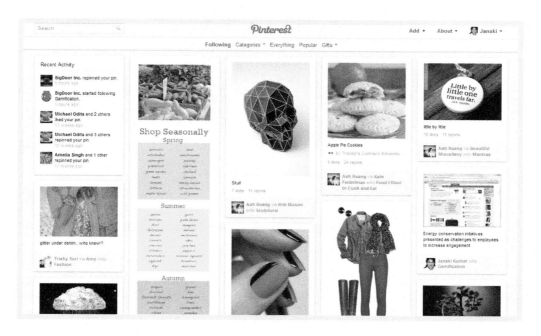

FIGURE 6.14: Aesthetics in visual design.

Copyright © Pinterest. All Rights Reserved. Used without permission under the Fair Use Doctrine. See the "Exceptions" section (and subsection "fairUse") of the copyright notice.

---

28. Norman, Don, 2005, Emotional Design - Why We Love (or Hate) Everyday Things, http://www.amazon.com/Emotional-Design-Love-Everyday-Things/dp/0465051367

Humor is another emotion pertinent to game mechanics. The tone of the product can be conveyed in the micro-copy, or in the informational text and messages on the user interfaces. Humor has the power to deflect a negative experience into a (somewhat) positive one.

Humorous micro-copy addresses the motivational driver of feedback, while people may choose to use esthetically pleasing designed products as an avenue of self-expression.

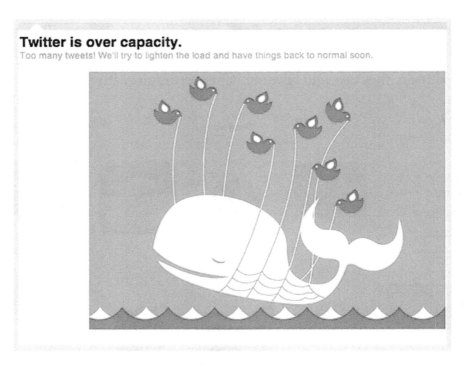

FIGURE 6.15: Twitter fail whale. Their website is down, and instead of being an-
            noyed, we smile.

Copyright © Twitter. All Rights Reserved. Used without permission under the Fair Use Doctrine. See the "Exceptions" section (and subsection "fairUse") of the copyright notice.

6.2 THE GAME PLAN

With a solid understanding of the player, mission, and motivation, the gamification system may be designed using game mechanics as building blocks. The three main considerations in pulling together the game plan are the game economy, game rules, engagement loops.

6.2.1 *Game Economy*

Garner describes game economy as follows:

There are four basic currencies that players accumulate in game economies — fun, things, social capital and self-esteem — that are implemented through game mechanics, such as points, badges and leaderboards. These game mechanics are simply tokens of different currencies of motivation that are being applied to reward players.

The Game Economy

Self Esteem	Fun
Leadership	Discovery
Conquest	Excitement
Mastery	Awe
Access	Delight
Praise	Fantasy
	Surprise

------ Levels ------ Badges ------

Social Capital		Things
Likes		Points
Friends		Cash
Contribute	Gifts	Resources
Charity		Rewards
Groups		Prices
Status		

FIGURE 6.16: Game Economy.

Courtesy of Janaki Kumar and Mario Herger. Copyright: CC-Att-ND (Creative Commons Attribution-NoDerivs 3.0 Unported).

Fun refers to rewards such as discovery, excitement, fantasy, awe, delight, and surprise. Things refer to cash, resources, and prizes or gifts. Social capital refers to likes, friends, and status. Self-esteem refers to praise, access, mastery, and conquest.

As part of the game plan, you can decide the mechanics you want to use as currencies in your game economy.

6.2.2 *Game Rules*

Once you have decided what mechanics to use, the next thing is to come up with a set of rules of the game. If you are designing a system to motivate call center employees to undergo training, and you have decided to use points in your game economy, you will need to decide how many points you award for the action. If the employee only took 50% of the training, do they receive all the points, none of the points, or 50% of the points?

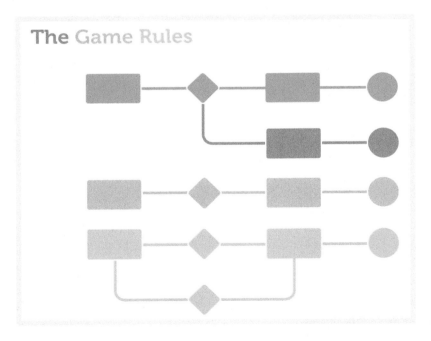

FIGURE 6.17: Game Rules.

If you are designing a community where you are trying to increase participation, do you award points for all comments, or only for thoughtful comments, and who decides if a comment is thoughtful?

The rules of the game pull together the mechanics into a flow to motivate the player to achieve the mission.

6.2.3 *Engagement Loop*

The core engagement loop refers to game mechanics combined with positive reinforcement and feedback loops that keep the player engaged in the game. This concept has been discussed by Amy Jo Kim[29], a renowned game designer.

The four main stages in the loop are:

- ► Motivate emotion,
- ► Call to action,
- ► Re-engage,
- ► Feedback and reward.

---

29. http://www.slideshare.net/amyjokim/gamification-101-design-the-player-journey67

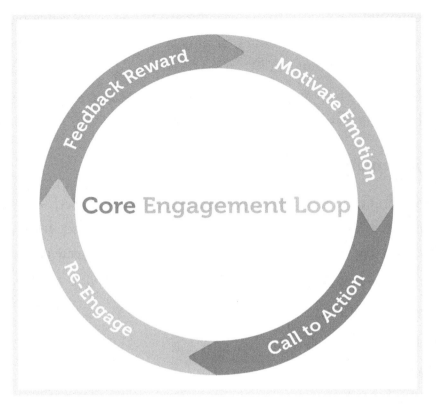

FIGURE 6.18: Core engagement loop.

Courtesy of Janaki Kumar and Mario Herger. Copyright: CC-Att-ND (Creative Commons Attribution-NoDerivs 3.0 Unported).

For example, a new player to a community site may:

- ▶ visit out of curiosity,

- ▶ participate via a challenge,

- ▶ be reminded by the system to check-in periodically to explore and discover new features,

- ▶ receive feedback and rewards for participation.

This frequent invitation to interact with the system creates positive reinforcement and the player will be motivated to stay engaged with the gamified system.

6.3 SUMMARY

Game mechanics are the most visible aspect of gamification. To be successful, mechanics need to be selected based on a thorough understanding of the player, the mission and human motivation.

In this chapter, we have presented a curated list of game mechanics that can help you start your journey into gamification. They are points, badges, leaderboards, relationships, challenges, constraints, journey, narrative, and emotion.

We guide you in creating a game plan that uses these mechanics as building blocks. The main elements to consider in the game plan are game economy, game rules, and the engagement loop.

The gamification system needs to engage the player continuously as part of a sustainable strategy.

6.4 INSIGHTS FROM SAP COMMUNITY NETWORK

In 2005, it was not common for communities to award points for participation. SCN ventured carefully into applying game mechanics by designing the system as follows:

▶ A regular blog post earned 40 points. Exceptional posts were awarded additional points while points were deducted for posts with short-comings

▶ Responses to questions were awarded between 2 and 10 points. Additional points were awarded for answers that were thoughtful or exceptional in solving the problem

▶ Points were awarded for wiki-edits depending on the amount of contribution.

▶ Badges were introduced to distinguish SAP employees. Community members could reach out to them directly to get more information from an SAP perspective.

▶ Members with administrative authority on forums and blogs were given Moderator badges.

▶ SCN offers leaderboards to showcase expertise in the community. The system also tracks life-time points for each player.

This simple combination of points, badges and leaderboards created a positive dynamic. However, it also led to some unintended consequences, which we will discuss in the next chapter.

To be continued at the end of next chapter...

Your notes and thoughts on chapter 6

Record your notes and thoughts on this chapter. If you want to share these thoughts with others online, go to the bottom of the page at: http://www.interaction-design.org/books/gamification_at_work/chapter_6_mechanics.html

NOTES:

_____

_____

_____

_____

_____

_____

_____

_____

CHAPTER

7

Manage, Monitor and Measure

"Gamification is not a project...
it's a program that gets invested in for the long-term.
Those that understand that see the most impactful and meaningful results."

— *Kris Duggan, Founder of gamification platform Badgeville*

7.1 CREATING A SUSTAINABLE GAMIFICATION STRATEGY

We recommend thinking of gamification as a program in your organization, rather than a project. Sustainable gamification takes long-term commitment and iteration to be successful.

Playtesting is the type of usability testing done by game design companies, where players are observed while they play with the product. Plan to playtest your gamification designs throughout the design process at different levels of fidelity before eventual rollout.

To ensure the success of your gamification efforts, the three essential aspects to consider are managing the mission, monitoring player motivation and measuring the metrics to fine- tune the gamification strategy continuously.

7.1.1 *Manage the mission*

Managing expectations with regard to the mission is an important aspect of ensuring success for your gamification efforts. Chapter 4 described how to identify a mission, and encouraged you to strive for SMART mission statements — specific, measurable, achievable, realistic, and time bound. Share the mission with everyone in the team to create a common vision. Periodically evaluate the validity of the mission and adjust if needed.

We recommend planning for a few releases looking into the future and not just for the immediate one. The mission could stay the same over multiple releases or be modified for each release. For example, in a community site, the mission for the first release is to encourage participation, and in a subsequent release, the mission may be focused around increasing quality of content.

7.1.2 *Monitor player motivation*

After the implementation of gamification, conduct qualitative research through observation or interviews to study the impact on player interaction, delight and motivation.

It is important to plan for player fatigue. When gamification is introduced, players may be engaged and delighted. However, as time goes by and the novelty wears off, player engagement and delight may go down as well.

One strategy to counter player fatigue is to plan for a few releases ahead and introduce new features periodically to sustain novelty and interest. A similar strategy is to consider the players' journeys and their level of expertise with regard to the gamified system. Introduce a small set of features in the beginning as the player is onboarding, and unlock more functions as the player acquires more skills.

Traditional games do this by allowing players to graduate to more challenging levels to keep them engaged. Amy Jo Kim, describes the Player Life Cycle with respect to game design. She refers to the players as Rookie, Regular or Master based on their expertise, and designs the game appropriately around their needs to avoid dropout.

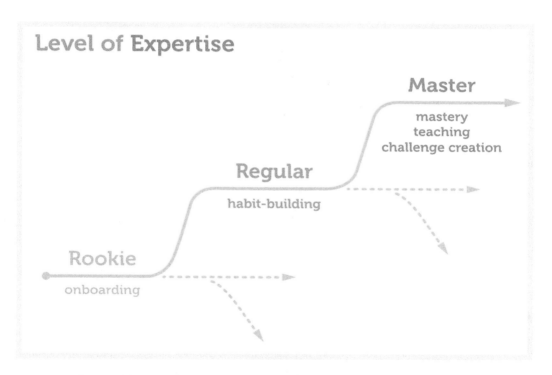

FIGURE 7.1: Player's life cycle by Amy Jo Kim.

Courtesy of Janaki Kumar and Mario Herger. Copyright: CC-Att-ND (Creative Commons Attribution-NoDerivs 3.0 Unported).

This means the team has to plan a roadmap of gamification features a few releases ahead, and not just the immediate one. They also need to consider the players' skill level to sustain their engagement and delight.

7.1.3 *Measure effectiveness of mechanics*

Brainstorm with the product team to identify the metrics i.e., the key performance indicators of gamification success. Then find a way to get this data. For your reference, here are a few examples of common metrics.

- ▶ Engagement
  - ◆ Average number of actions
  - ◆ Median number of actions
  - ◆ Number of users performing actions
  - ◆ Number of times users return
  - ◆ Progression of users through the experience
  - ◆ Customer satisfaction results
- ▶ Time
  - ◆ Retention
  - ◆ Frequency
  - ◆ Decrease of response time
  - ◆ Timeliness
- ▶ ROI
  - ◆ Number of active users
  - ◆ Productivity increase
  - ◆ Cost reductions
  - ◆ Sales increase
- ▶ Quality
  - ◆ Article ratings — in case of community site

+ Fields filled out — in case of sales automation tool where the mission is to encourage sales reps to enter data completely for accurate reporting

Be selective in identifying the metric since it requires data collection. Note that the more data you collect the more storage and processing requirements you generate. Big data is a topic that is relevant to gamification. Plan for big data, and consider the performance impact on the players.

7.2 TIPS FOR SUCCESS IN A CORPORATE SETTING

There are some special aspects to gamification in a corporate setting and some tips to help you.

7.2.1 *Get a gamification sponsor*

Identify an executive in the company to sponsor your gamification efforts. This has many benefits. First, it gives you a budget to work with. We will discuss why this is necessary below. Secondly, there is still a stigma attached to playing at work. Employees not familiar with gamification may be skeptical, and you might end up spending much time countering this skepticism. Getting an endorsement from a high level executive can help your case, since you can use these executives as enlightened role models.

Of course, executive sponsorship is always a two-way street. Once you get a sponsor, you will need to keep your sponsor regularly updated on your activities in addition to sharing your success stories and lessons learnt. This has the additional benefit of indirectly recruiting an executive to be your public relations spokesperson in meetings in which he or she is present and you are not.

7.2.2 *Budget*

Here are a few line items you will need to consider as part of your gamification budget:

- ▶ Creating the gamification experience
  - ◆ Game designers
  - ◆ Graphic designers
  - ◆ Developers
- ▶ Maintaining the game
  - ◆ Admins
  - ◆ Support
  - ◆ IT
  - ◆ Prizes/Rewards
  - ◆ Updating the game
  - ◆ New Missions/Challenges
  - ◆ Adding Challenge Levels
  - ◆ Gamification Platform license fees

7.2.3 *Prepare for rollout*

There are two strategies for rollout.

7.2.3.1 Big-bang rollout

This involves a standard software maker rolling out gamification to all customers, or the entire user base for internal teams. To do this successfully, the team will need to invest in publicity and marketing of gamification to gain support. There is a risk and cost associated with this approach. We do not recommend this unless you and the product team have a high level of confidence in the gamification strategy.

7.2.3.2 Start with a pilot, monitor results and roll out slowly

For first releases of gamification, the recommended approach is to start with a pilot, gather feedback from players, and roll out in phases. This is a less risky strategy.

7.2.4 *Opt in or mandatory?*

If participation in gamification is mandatory, it will take the fun out of it. Players should be able to able to stop playing at any time. In the chapter on Legal and Ethical considerations, we will elaborate on labor laws that protect employees in some countries.

7.2.5 *"Hello help desk? My points are missing!"*

Employees and customers have different set of expectations when they are interacting with consumer software or enterprise software. If a person uses a consumer website that offers some gamification points and badges, and if some of the points are lost due to a technical glitch, the consumer may be annoyed briefly, but will move on. If an employee has earned points for technical expertise and if those points are lost due to a technical error, the employee may go beyond mere annoyance and call HR to complain. Plan for such scenarios with data backup and rollback.

During early releases of the product, when the platform is still maturing, such backup and restore services may not yet be available. In such cases, make players aware that the company cannot provide any guarantees for their points earned in the current release, and allow them to opt out at any time.

7.3 SUMMARY

Once you have developed a gamification strategy and implemented it, you are not done. You have just begun. In this chapter, we point out ways to create a holistic and sustainable gamification strategy for the enterprise. We also provide some practical advice pertinent to a corporate setting.

7.4 INSIGHTS FROM SAP COMMUNITY NETWORK

To make SCN successful, administrators have established some rules and metrics, and monitor the activities of the community.

Rules

▶ All players are required to treat each other with respect and with courtesy.

▶ New users were required to learn by following the forums, browsing the blogs, and using the search tool before asking a question.

▶ More experienced users can blog and access advanced features of SCN.

Metrics

Metrics that were monitored changed over time. The most common were:

▶ Number of registered users

▶ Number of active users<

▶ Number of top contributors (above a certain point threshold per period)

▶ Average response times to forum questions

▶ Other metrics like the Net Promoter Score, which is a measure of the satisfaction of members in the community.

Monitoring

Monitoring was not restricted to quantitative metrics. Administrators and moderators (community members who had earned the status of moderator) proactively monitored the community and focused on the quality of the discussion. They enforced the agreed upon SCN rules by punishing rule-breakers and cheaters.

Cheating

Whenever there are rules, and benefits to be gained, cheating will happen. It was no surprise that some members of the SCN also tried to cheat the system to earn more points. One of the most common forms of cheating is when a member creates multiple accounts, asks a question with one name, and responds with another name. Both the questions and the answers were often very simple and a repetition of information that was already available on the SCN. Regular SCN members felt that this was a dilution of content on the community that made searching for helpful information more difficult. This led to regular members voluntarily taking on the role of governance. They developed a sharp eye to identify such behavior, and they reported such incidents to the SCN administrators who either warned the offending member or suspended them.

This shows that rules need to be enforced to keep the community valuable for compliant members who form the majority of any community.

Positive reinforcement

SCN administrators proactively rewarded good behavior and sought ways to enrich the SCN experience. For example, players who reached a point threshold received a t-shirt with their SCN points printed on them. Members proudly wore it at SAP events and locally organized SCN events as status symbols. Eventually this practice was discontinued because the community proposed SAP could donate the money to charity on their behalf.

Unintended Consequences

The community members' employers started to monitor their employees' activities on SCN. Due to the openness of the system, they could easily keep track of the number of contributions, as well as their quality.

Consulting companies would publicize their employees' SCN ranking to promote their services. This led some companies to incentivize employees to contribute by adding this as an objective to their performance evaluation. Companies that needed experts on their projects, staffed them by searching for them on SCN. Hiring managers indicated that they preferred candidates who listed their SCN point score on their resumes. Through SCN, they could examine the quality and rating of the contributions, since the track record is publicly available. This raises some legal and ethical questions, which we will examine in the next chapter.

To be continued at the end of next chapter...

YOUR NOTES AND THOUGHTS ON CHAPTER 7

Record your notes and thoughts on this chapter. If you want to share these thoughts with others online, go to the bottom of the page at: http://www.interaction-design.org/books/gamification_at_work/chapter_7_manage_monitor_and_measure.html

NOTES:

CHAPTER
8

Legal and Ethical Considerations

"If you use the power of games to give people an opportunity to do something they want to do, then you're doing good. If you're using the power of games to get people to do something you want them to do, then you're doing evil."

— *Jane McGonigal*

When gamification enters the enterprise, the laws and regulations governing businesses apply to gamification as well, with severe consequences for non-compliance. Here are a few legal and ethical considerations that affect gamification in the work place. We recommend consulting your company's legal department (since neither author is a lawyer), to ensure that your gamification endeavors do not inadvertently violate any laws or ethics, such as labor laws, data privacy, etc.

8.1 LEGAL CONSIDERATIONS

When creating global business software, it is important to consider not only the laws of your country, but all countries your software will be implemented in. This is indeed a daunting challenge with high probability of and consequences for error. Therefore, we recommend a flexible and configurable gamification design that provides rich capability for your customers to turn features on or off based on their regional policies or preferences.

8.1.1 *Labor laws*

Labor laws and employee protections vary across the world. Generally, in European countries like Germany there are many laws in place to protect employees. In addition, unions[30] exist even for white-collar office workers. These unions or workers' councils are allowed to interpret the laws[31] in order to maximize protection for the employee population. Traditionally, data collection about the employee is strictly monitored by workers' councils. They pay attention to the following questions:

▶ What is the purpose of data collection and is the amount of collected data justified?

▶ Where is the data stored?

▶ Can the same purpose be reached with less data as well

▶ Is the data anonymized or can it be assigned to individual employees?

▶ Does the data serve as a basis for performance review decisions — and therefore influence decisions on salary increase, bonus calculations, promotions or layoffs?

---

30. Betriebsverfassungsgesetz http://www.gesetze-im-internet.de/betrvg/__87.html

31. Such rights are listed in § 87 (1) of the German Corporate Code (Betriebsverfassungsgesetz). The implementation and application of technical systems that can be used for behavior- and performance-control require the approval from the workers council, as well as all aspects around corporate salary structures.

These laws have a direct impact on gamification, since features such as leaderboards will need workers' council approval in each company. The council will need to be satisfied that such leaderboards will have no negative impact on an employee's performance review, wages or salary, or bonus plan.

Plan time in the schedule for such approval cycles and design the system in a way that gamification features (such as leaderboards) may be "turned off" if not approved, so as not to jeopardize the entire product release.

8.1.2 *Data privacy laws*

Data privacy laws vary globally as well. Generally, European laws forbid the collection, processing, and use of personally identifiable data, unless other laws and regulations explicitly permit or order it, or if the person involved gives his or her permission for such collection and processing of personal data.[32]

If the gamified system will be rolled out in countries with such protection, employees and customers should explicitly opt-in to have data collected on their behalf. Therefore, the default setting needs to be opt-out, so that the employee or customer must explicitly perform an action (sign a document, click a button or check a check box) to agree to their personal data being collected and used.

8.1.3 *Virtual currencies and banking laws*

There are many legal challenges and restrictions with regard to virtual currencies and assets.[33] The main discussions and the applicable laws and regulations circulate around these four questions:

1. How was the virtual currency / asset acquired?
2. How was it used?

---

32. Example: German federal privacy law §4 BDSG

33. For more information see James Gatto's Gamification Law: Formula for Success video at http://vimeo.com/30579380

3. When was it used?

4. Who used it?

There are a few examples of lawsuits involving operators of virtual worlds and currencies pertinent to gamification in the enterprise, such as Linden Lab and their SecondLife (Virtual Land Dispute,[34] Class Action Virtual Land Dispute,)[35] or of social game companies like Zynga (Poker Chip Theft).[36]

Since the economic crisis of 2008, a number of stricter regulations have been introduced to offer more consumer protection, which regulates providers of financial services.

The main impact on gamification relates to the types of reward that may be offered as part of the gamified system. Could the player trade their virtual points with other players? Challenges such as virtual betting may be governed by gambling laws and state monopoly laws may apply.

8.1.4 *Data ownership*

Who owns the data? The answer to this question is still evolving in the courts. For example, Facebook has had to change its terms of use[37] in Europe based on lawsuits.

In the enterprise context, if an employee earns frequent flier points while taking business trips on behalf of the company, to whom do the points belong? Generally accepted business etiquette is to allow the points to belong to the employee but this is not a guarantee. In a professional community, if an employee earns points for their expertise, the company they work for directly or indirectly

34. http://arstechnica.com/tech-policy/2007/06/second-life-land-dispute-moves-offline-to-federal-court-room/

35. http://mashable.com/2010/05/03/second-life-users-file-class-action-lawsuit-over-virtual-land/

36. http://www.gamespot.com/news/brit-jailed-over-zynga-poker-chip-theft-6305366

37. http://www.gamespot.com/news/brit-jailed-over-zynga-poker-chip-theft-6305366

benefits from the employee's ranking in the leaderboard. If the employee were suddenly to lose this ranking, will this affect the company as well?

In summary, we recommend a conservative approach to data ownership, especially since the laws are still evolving. Employees and customers must have a say in what information is collected on their behalf, who sees the data, what is the purpose of this data collection, how much data is collected, and they must be allowed to opt out if they so choose (and in Europe, encouraged to opt-in, with opt-out being the default setting).

8.2 ETHICAL CONSIDERATIONS

Manuel Velasquez, Claire Andre, Thomas Shanks, S.J., and Michael J. Meyer from the Santa Clara University in California[38] define ethics as follows:

"Ethics refers to well-founded standards of right and wrong that prescribe what humans ought to do, usually in terms of rights, obligations, benefits to society, fairness, or specific virtues."

This applies to gamification as well, and players need to be treated ethically, fairly and with respect.

Gamification is not a substitute for fair compensation policies. If employees are not paid fairly in accordance with market standards for the job they do, no amount of gamification will make them motivated at work.

8.2.1 *Manipulating vs. Nudging*

As Adena DeMonte, of Badgeville puts it:

"[..] gamification can never be successful exploitationware, because it only works when the behaviors that are motivated are behaviors that the user wants to

---

38. What is Ethics?
http://www.scu.edu/ethics/practicing/decision/whatisethics.html

perform in the first place. It's not some magic solution where you can manipulate users to perform behaviors against their will."

However, economist Richard Thaler and legal scholar Cass Sunstein, in their book *Nudge Improving Decisions about Health, Wealth, and Happiness,*[39] argue successfully that it is possible to encourage or nudge people to make "good" choices. Positioning fruits at the beginning and unhealthier food items at a remote position in a cafeteria, or setting the default option for choosing a health care plan to a government selected one, or setting the default to donate organs (instead of the other way round), are ways in which people can be supported to make better choices.

As gamification designers, we are social architects to some degree, and we need to take this responsibility seriously. Gamification in the workplace connects the virtual world to the real world, and decisions players make in the gamified system affect their real life outside the system. So use this power for good! Reminding players to recycle and turn off the light is using the power for good. While forcing people to purchase products and services they do not need using in-game purchase screens that will not go away, or making players' rights confusing and incomprehensible to them using legal mumbo-jumbo are examples of using this power for evil.

8.2.2 *Player Cheating*

We have news for you — there will be players who will cheat or try to cheat your gamified system[40]. However, your job is to minimize the cheating and build a relatively cheat-resistant system to make it enjoyable for all players.

---

39. Richard Thaler, Cass Sunstein, Nudge: Improving Decisions about Health, Wealth, and Happiness, Yale University Press, 2008

40. Michael Wu's blog: http://lithosphere.lithium.com/t5/Building-Community-the-Platform/Beat-the-Cheat-Stop-Gaming-the-Gamification/ba-p/30887 http://lithosphere.lithium.com/t5/Building-Community-the-Platform/Relatively-Cheat-Resistant-Rewards-and-Metrics-for-Gamification/ba-p/30889

There are three strategies to reduce cheating.

- ▶ Decreasing the perceived value of rewards
    - ◆ Use intrinsic rewards without transferable value in the real world
    - ◆ Use perks with low exchangeable value
    - ◆ Use rewards that have a large perceived-value differential between the target audience and the rest of the world
- ▶ Increasing the effort required to game the system (no pun intended!)
    - ◆ Make combination of rewards metrics so complex, that gaming it cannot be understood (Google PageRank)
    - ◆ Metrics that are less susceptible to gaming
    - ◆ Time-bounded, unique-user-based reciprocity metrics (or TUUR metrics) -> e.g. # of Retweets
    - ◆ Time-bounded, unique-content-based reciprocity metrics (or TUCR metric) -> e.g. # of Likes
    - ◆ Total transparency and social shame and or accountability

8.3 SUMMARY

Gamification is emerging as a strategic business practice. Gamification of global business software raises a number of challenging questions with regard to regional differences in laws and business practices. In this chapter, we provide an overview to the legal and ethical factors to consider as part of your gamified system. We recommend consulting with a qualified legal professional in your organization to alert you to potential issues you may not have considered to ensure the success of your overall gamification strategy.

8.4 INSIGHTS FROM SAP COMMUNITY NETWORK

Since SCN is a globally and publicly accessible community, legal disclaimers, terms of use, and data privacy statements needed to be implemented on a regional basis. For example, were the points earned by players solely their own, or did their employers have any claim to them?

In certain regions like Europe, more restrictive data privacy laws had to be considered. Players must actively opt-in to have their information made public, and to be able to participate fully in the community.

SCN worked with SAP's legal department to create documents to clarify content ownership, content standards, usage, responsibility in case of disputes, data privacy, etc. We continue to keep a watchful eye on the community to ensure it is a safe place for developers to thrive.

The end

Your notes and thoughts on chapter 8

Record your notes and thoughts on this chapter. If you want to share these thoughts with others online, go to the bottom of the page at: http://www.interaction-design.org/books/gamification_at_work/chapter_8_legal_and_ethical_considerations.html

NOTES:

CHAPTER

9

Enterprise Gamification Examples

"Gamification is as important as social and mobile."

— *Bing Gordon, partner at Kleiner Perkins*

Gamification is still an emerging concept in the enterprise, so we do not have access to longitudinal studies on its effectiveness. The following examples are to provide inspiration for your own gamification endeavors.

9.1 PERSONAL SUSTAINABILITY

In 2010, our team in SAP Labs Palo Alto conducted research on personal sustainability - in collaboration between Aaron Marcus and Associates - as part of building a suite of sustainability applications. The intended users of these personal sustainability products were the employees of companies who purchase these products. It allows employees and potentially customers and partners to contribute to the sustainability key performance metrics of the company through their individual actions.

We interviewed more than 100 people to explore their attitudes and reactions to sustainability, identifed key areas of concern, determined what motivated people to take personal action, and examined the language used around sustainability.

We conducted four types of research activities:

► Media Content Analysis: The goal was to determine which issues recieved popular attention and what language was used in the media. We reviewed top media sources of sustainability news, generated tag clouds of most used words and tracked attitudes towards issues as well as the frequency of their appearance in the media.

► "Man on the Street" user interviews: The goal was to get spontaneous reactions to sustainability, language used, top issues of concern, and potential geographical variance. We interviewed people in three different locations — San Francisco, Walnut Creek, and Berkeley. Subjects were interviewed at their work or when shopping. Each participant was asked the same five questions about their personal experience and opinions about sustainability. The questions were:

♦ There is a lot of talk in the news and media right now about sustainability and related issues. What do you think of that? What does sustainability mean to you?

♦ Do you have personal concerns about any particular issues regarding sustainability?

♦ Have you personally made any changes in your life around your sustainability concerns? Is there anything that you would like to do?

- ♦ Did you have any resources that helped you make those changes or prompted you to make those changes, and if so, what were they and how did you make those changes?

- ♦ Is there anything that you read or hear about regarding the topic that seems silly to you?

▶ Focus Groups: The goal was to elicit thoughtful responses from the participants. The same five questions were distributed to focus group participants the day before the group session. The focus group sessions were conducted with roughly ten participants each.

▶ Surveys: The goal was to test the consistency or differences in international responses, and to see trends in attitudes from large sampling of participants. The survey was distributed internationally, containing the same five questions. Responses were received from 76 respondents in 17 countries.

A set of design principles emerged from this research. They were:

▶ Fit into their daily lives: Focus on what users do, not what they say they care about. During the user research, people say they have high level concerns — environmental degradation, peak oil, wasteful consumer culture — but actions they report actually taking occur during daily life, *e.g.*, recycling, biking, taking public transit, buying organic & locally grown food.

▶ Motivate effectively: Allow users to calculate financial benefit easily; do not nag and avoid polarizing viewpoint.

▶ Leverage community influence: Promote community building, allow community to coerce sustainable behavior within reason and avoid appearing too authoritative.

▶ Build trust: Facilitate knowledge sharing among friends and communities, and provide transparency.

▶ Leverage persuasion theory[41] and gamification: Promote competition, reward success, give clear actionable recommendations and avoid general obvious ones.

Based on these design principles, the team designed a set of scenarios and mini-applications.

The overall mission was to engage employees in the sustainability initiatives of the company. We created the concept of initiatives that leaders in the community could initiate and draw others into the cause.

One of the concepts that the team created to illustrate the concept of Initiatives is called Vampire Hunter. Vampires are energy suckers that utilize energy even when they are turned off. Vampire energy is estimated to cost U.S, consumers $3 billion a year.[42] Vampire energy reduction results in cost savings and greenhouse gas reduction.

To address this use case, the team designed a game called the Vampire Hunter where departments, buildings and regional offices could compete to identify and reduce such vampire energy wastage in corporate settings.

41. D, O'Keefe. 2002. Persuasion: Theory and Research

42. http://energy.gov/energysaver/articles/vampire-power-scary-all-year-round Department of Energy

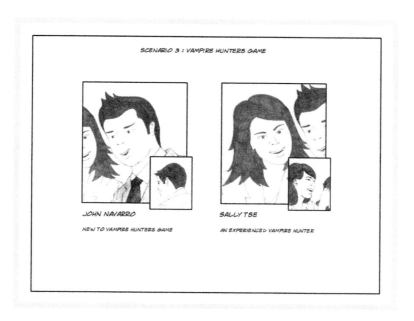

FIGURE 9.1: Vampire Hunter storyboard - the players.

Courtesy of Mario Herger. Copyright: CC-Att-ND (Creative Commons Attribution-NoDerivs 3.0 Unported).

FIGURE 9.2: Vampire Hunter storyboard - the initiative.

Courtesy of Mario Herger. Copyright: CC-Att-ND (Creative Commons Attribution-NoDerivs 3.0 Unported).

FIGURE 9.3: Vampire Hunter storyboard - the community.

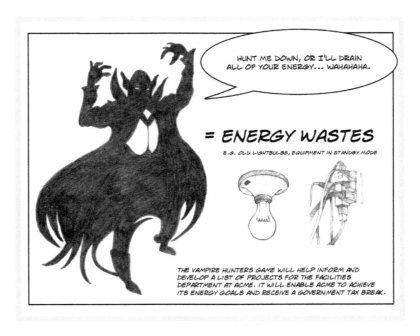

FIGURE 9.4: Vampire Hunter storyboard - Vampires are energy suckers.

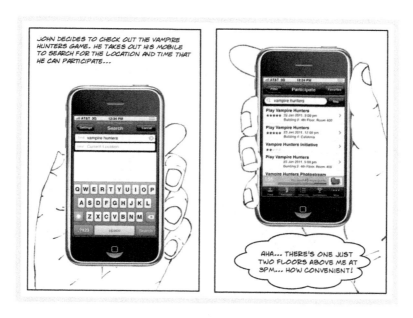

FIGURE 9.5: Vampire Hunter storyboard - mobile interactions.

FIGURE 9.6: Vampire Hunter storyboard - the real community and the virtual community.

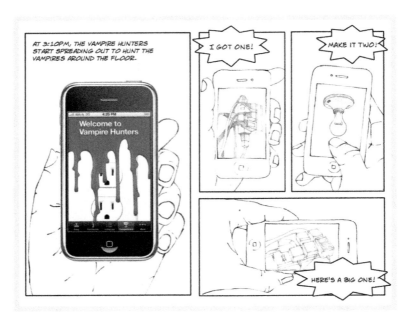

FIGURE 9.7: Vampire Hunter storyboard - got one!.

Courtesy of Mario Herger. Copyright: CC-Att-ND (Creative Commons Attribution-NoDerivs 3.0 Unported).

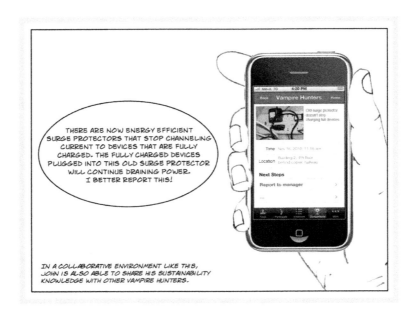

FIGURE 9.8: Vampire Hunter storyboard - share knowledge with community.

Courtesy of Mario Herger. Copyright: CC-Att-ND (Creative Commons Attribution-NoDerivs 3.0 Unported).

FIGURE 9.9: Vampire Hunter storyboard - map view.

Courtesy of Mario Herger. Copyright: CC-Att-ND (Creative Commons Attribution-NoDerivs 3.0 Unported).

FIGURE 9.10: Vampire Hunter storyboard - leaderboard.

Courtesy of Mario Herger. Copyright: CC-Att-ND (Creative Commons Attribution-NoDerivs 3.0 Unported).

Employees form teams and compete to identify "vampires" — or in more prosaic terms: "products that waste energy" — on the corporate campus.

They join the "vampire hunt" — a type of scavenger hunt — where colleagues walk through a certain area of a building to identify old light bulbs, equipment in standby mode, old surge protectors that keep charging devices even if they are fully charged, and other energy suckers. They take pictures with their smartphones and report that to the "vampire hunter headquarters." For each vampire found, a total of saved kWh is calculated and awarded to the members. The result leads not only to a reduction in energy consumption, lower costs and potential tax breaks, but also encourages previously unacquainted colleagues to network with one another.

9.2 SAP ROADWARRIOR

Being a sales representative in a large technology company like SAP involves keeping up with a constant stream of new technical information and dynamic changes. Sales representatives in emerging areas such as mobility technology have noted that they feel "sandwiched" between the inquiries and questions from customers and the flood of new technologies and mobile applications released by the development teams.

Typically, there are documents and e-learning videos available to the sales reps. However, these are time-consuming to go through, and sales reps do not find that this training format meets their needs.

Enter SAP Roadwarrior! SAP Roadwarrior is a game that simulates a customer meeting in which the sales rep needs to respond to customer questions to earn points and unlock badges. First, the sales rep is offered company information as part of a "pre-call planning". Then the sales reps are presented a series of customer questions. They can earn points and badges and unlock levels for correct question and meeting preparation. In the background, the system creates a "cheat sheet", for the sales rep, which the sales rep could use for real customer meetings. The game has features such as "life line" which allows the sales rep to learn throughout the game. It also offers instant feedback via a "conversation meter", to show how well the meeting is going.

FIGURE 9.11: SAP Roadwarrior screen showing the simulated sales negotiation with the CTO of a car auctioning company.

Sales reps meet with several customers in one industry before they can unlock the next level to meet customers from other industries. This allows sales reps to gather cross-industry knowledge. Players can also challenge other players, to match answers to a question. A leaderboard shows the score of all players. Being competitive in nature, this motivates the sales reps to try to do better than their peers do. Ultimately, it helps them feel more comfortable in customer meetings, having practiced via the simulations in Roadwarrior.

In the end, this game fulfills three purposes: it turns learning about SAP's mobile applications and technologies into a fun game, it puts sales reps into simulated meetings with customers to prepare them for real meetings, and it allows players to socialize, compete with and motivate each other. Of course, the real goal of the player is to sell more, make more money, and retire by 35 on an island in the Caribbean. "Another piña colada for the Beachwarrior, please!"

9.3 TIME RECORDING

Recently, at the Gamification Summit in San Francisco, one of the authors (Herger) met Brady Wicken from the consulting company Slalom Consulting. He shared a gamified version of a time recording system that they had implemented in their organization.

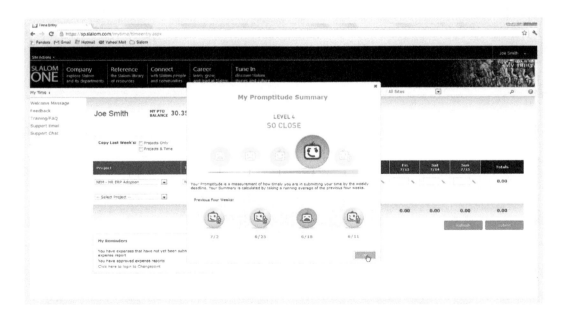

FIGURE 9.12: Time Recording.

Slalom Consulting is a company that requires all their employees to assign their time correctly and promptly to the clients for accurate and on-time billing. The time must be entered by Sunday, approved by managers on Monday, clients billed and payroll run by Wednesday.

Any delay on the part of the employee delays the entire process downstream. To encourage employees to enter their time by Sunday, they created a "Promptitude" score. This is a simple score that evaluates if the employee entered their time by Sunday noon PST, and calculates a 4-week running average. This score is displayed on a scale of 1 — 5 with a sense of humor. The lowest score has some hilarious text that incorporates a healthy dose of friendly "Shamification". Introducing this simple widget was enough to remind the employees and motivate them to enter their information in time.

9.4 SMARTGATE — THE CHANGE MANAGEMENT GAME

In 2009 Air Cargo Netherlands, Dutch Customs and Schiphol Airport decided to improve collaboration within the logistics chain to increase speed of deliveries. The logistics chain refers to the management of the flow of resources from its point of origin to its destination. It includes the process steps involved in both the flow of physical goods and the information flow in the system. To smoothen the airfreight system, they introduced a system called SmartGate[43] to have all parties in the logistics chain share relevant information in time. To educate employees from the parties involved, a game-version of SmartGate was developed that helped with the change management process to onboard people faster and make them feel more comfortable with the new system.

The objectives were to introduce SmartGate as a new way of working, to increase insight in 'chain-thinking' and show the consequences of transporting

---

43. http://www.smartgatethegame.nl

'green' and 'red' freight. The target audience was 350 companies surrounding Schiphol Airport, involved in the air cargo industry as either a shipper, forwarder, trucker, handler, or airline.

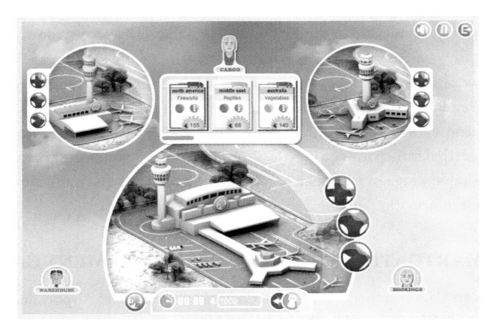

FIGURE 9.13: Smart Gate for change management and training.

9.5 COMPLIANCE TRAINING

Employees of large corporations are required to complete mandatory compliance training annually. At SAP, we go through an online version of the Corporate Security and Business Code of conduct training. We are then tested on our knowledge and certified to be in compliance. Managers need to complete the Sexual Harassment[44] training periodically as well. Companies need to report externally the level to which their employees are trained and certified.

---

44. On a side note, should it not be called Anti-Sexual Harassment training?

Most employees understand such compliance training's importance and business value, but find it boring and time consuming. As a result, a number of employees procrastinate and forget to complete the training. This leads to multiple reminders and managers being notified on non-compliance. This is all around a painful process for all parties concerned.

This is where TrueOffice comes in. The creative staff of TrueOffice have turned this boring compliance process round and gamified it. The players are normal office workers, and the mission is to train them and certify them in compliance. The designers have reimagined the dull compliance rules into fast-paced 20-minute interactive story modules. After each segment, the player is presented a compliance puzzle that they need to solve based on the training they just received. Players earn points and proceed through levels until completion.

Figure 9.14: Interviewing characters during a TrueOffice compliance training.

Managers can monitor their team's progress via a dash board. C-level executives can see their overall company's compliance status. TrueOffice is very popular in the banking industry as well as in other industries where a number of laws and regulations need strict compliance.

In January 2013, TruOffice raised $3.1 million in series A funding for gamified compliance training[45]. True Office Founder and CEO, Adam Sodowick made the following comment with regard to his company's funding:

"With fines now exceeding the billion dollar mark for compliance oversights, financial institutions are looking to True Office to provide a solution that not only protects their business and reduces costs, but also exponentially raises the current industry standard for compliance training. There aren't many effective options to help understand regulation and change behaviors but a well-designed game has the power to engage employees and at the same time, produce analytics that can help the banks identify and reduce operational and compliance risk."

9.6 MORE EXAMPLES

More gamification examples in the enterprise context can be found under http://enterprise-gamification.com/index.php/en/examples.

---

45. http://www.gamification.co/2013/01/24/trueoffice-raises-3m-in-series-a-funding-for-gamified-compliance-training/

YOUR NOTES AND THOUGHTS ON CHAPTER 9

Record your notes and thoughts on this chapter. If you want to share these thoughts with others online, go to the bottom of the page at: http://www.interaction-design.org/books/gamification_at_work/chapter_9_enterprise_gamification_examples.html

NOTES:

CHAPTER
10

Leveling Up

"Live and learn. Live to learn."

— Chinese saying

10.1 GURUS

There are a number of gamification and game design experts who regularly contribute to the community via blog posts, videos, slides, interviews and tweets. We recommend you subscribe to them to continue your ongoing education and to be inspired. Here is our collection, in no particular order:

▶ Gabe Zichermann

▶ Amy Jo Kim

▶ Sebastian Deterding

- ▶ Byron Reeves
- ▶ Marigo Raftapolous
- ▶ Kris Duggan
- ▶ Rajat Paharia
- ▶ Kevin Werbach
- ▶ Jane McGonigal
- ▶ Jesse Schell
- ▶ Jon Radoff
- ▶ Dan Pink
- ▶ Mihaly Csikzentmihaly
- ▶ Andrzej Marczewski
- ▶ Tyler Altrup
- ▶ Roman Rackwitz
- ▶ Toby Beresford
- ▶ Bart Hufen
- ▶ Mike Martoccia

To get the latest list of active gamification experts, follow the Gamification Guru Leaderboard, meticulously maintained by Toby Beresford: http://www.leader-boarded.com/gurus

10.2 BOOKS

The following is a selection of books on gamification, game design, learning and education, and motivation and behavior science.

10.2.1 *Gamification*

Mario Herger, *Enterprise Gamification — Exploiting people by letting them have fun;* CreateSpace, 2013

The bible of gamification at work for the serious gamification-designer, with over 450 pages, 200 enterprise gamification examples, and much more.

Gabe Zichermann and Christopher Cunningham: *Gamification by Design*; O'Reilly, 2011

A perfect practitioner guide for getting started with gamification.

Jane McGonigal: *Reality is Broken: Why Games Make Us Better and How They Can Change the World*; The Penguin Press, 2011

If you are new to gamification and want to get inspired, this is the book to start with. After reading it, you want to know more about the power of games in a real world context.

Michael Hugos: *Enterprise Games — Using Game Mechanics to Build a Better Business*; O'Reilly, 2012

Michael Hugos wrote the first comprehensible, and fact-based book on gamification in the corporate world.

Bryon Reeves and J. Leighton Read: *Total Engagement: Using Games and Virtual Worlds to Change the Way People Work and Businesses Compete*; Harvard Business Press, 2009

In this book, the authors discussed games in enterprises, before the term gamification was coined. They explain why games work in corporations, and offer some great examples.

Kevin Werbach and Dan Hunter: *For the Win: How Game Thinking Can Revolutionize Your Business*; Wharton Digital Press, 2012

Professors Kevin Werbach (of Coursera-fame) and Dan Hunter give an introduction to the use of gamification in work processes.

10.2.2 *Game Design*

Jesse Schell: *The Art of Game Design*; Morgan Kaufmann, 2008

One of the best books ever! Funny, self-deprecating, but very knowledgeable and fantastically written. This and the Deck of Lenses is a must for every game and gamification designer.

Jon Radoff: *Game On: Energize Your Business with Social Media Games*; Wiley, 2011

Jon Radoff offers a deep analysis of what makes games fun; the book is relevant for gamification.

10.2.3 *Learning & Education*

Karl M. Kapp: *The Gamification of Learning and Instruction*; Pfeiffer, 2012

If you are in the training and education space, this book is a must read. It shows how education and training in both schools/universities and corporations will change, and why.

Lee Sheldon: *The Multiplayer Classroom — Designing Courseworks as a Game*; Course Technology, 2012

Great example of how game designer Lee Sheldon, teaching video game design, uses game mechanics and game design to gamify the classroom experience.

It is a work in progress, so we expect to read more follow-ups on this. The book also contains a number of experiences from other teachers applying similar approaches to their classrooms. Also great results and facts quoted.

10.2.4 *Motivation & Behavioral Science*

Daniel Pink: *Drive: The Surprising Truth About What Motivates Us;* Riverhead Books, 2009

Dan Pink brings a number of examples that contradict conventional wisdom. For example that monetary rewards for creative tasks may decrease rather than increase employee engagement. Autonomy, mastery and purpose are much better motivators for innovation.

Charles Duhigg: *The Power of Habit: Why We Do What We Do in Life and Business*; Random House, 2012

An interesting introduction to how habits are formed and how they can be changed. Perfect for gamification designers, who want to change the habits of their users.

10.3 GAMIFICATION WEBSITES

Beside books, a number of websites and blogs publish a wealth of insights on gamification. Some are operated by gamification experts, some by organizations and the gamification industry. Here is a collection of gamification websites:

- ▶ http://www.enterprise-gamification.com/
- ▶ http://www.gamification.co/
- ▶ http://www.gamification.org/
- ▶ http://www.gamifiedenterprise.com/

▶ http://www.gamifeye.com/

▶ http://www.codingconduct.cc/

10.4 GAMIFICATION COMMUNITIES

Professional communities offer a place for gamification practitioners to connect with one another. Here are a few examples:

▶ http://www.gamificationcommunity.com

▶ http://scn.sap.com/community/gamification

▶ Sub- cummunities / or groups within:

▶ LinkedIn — http://www.linkedin.com

▶ XING — http://www.xing.com

▶ Facebook — http://www.facebook.com

10.5 GAMIFICATION CONFERENCES

There are a number of conferences and events dedicated to gamification and more conferences are adding gamification to their agenda.

The Gamification Community maintains a full list of gamification related events:

▶ http://www.gamificationcommunity.com/events

Here are a few highlights:

10.5.1 *North America*

▶ Gamification Summit — http://www.gsummit.com/

▶ Game Developer Conference — http://www.gdc.com/

- Games for Change — http://www.gamesforchange.org/
- Serious Play Conference — http://www.seriousplayconference.com/

10.5.2 *Europe, Middle East, Africa (EMEA)*

- Gamification Experience Europe — http://www.gamificationexperienceeurope.com/
- Social Business — http://socialbusiness.co.il/
- Gamification Symposium

10.5.3 *Asia, Pacific, Japan (APJ)*

- Gamification Conference Japan — http://gconference.jp/
- Our best wishes to you in your journey towards gamification mastery.

YOUR NOTES AND THOUGHTS ON CHAPTER 10

Record your notes and thoughts on this chapter. If you want to share these thoughts with others online, go to the bottom of the page at: http://www.interaction-design.org/books/gamification_at_work/chapter_10_leveling_up.html

NOTES:

_____

_____

_____

_____

_____

_____

_____

CHAPTER
11

Curated List of
Research techniques

Since this book is intended for both designers and non-designers, we offer you a brief description of a curated list of research techniques. Our objective is not to turn our readers into expert user researchers, since we strongly recommend including a professional user experience researcher as part of the enterprise gamification team. We introduce a curated list of user research and market research techniques pertinent to gamification in an enterprise context. Each of these techniques could be used individually or in combination, based on your objectives. We also refer you to additional references to go beyond the basics.

11.1 OBSERVATION

This technique focuses on seeing what the users actually do as opposed to what they say they do.

11.1.1 *Site visit / Field research*

This refers to research conducted outside a traditional lab setting, in a user's natural work environment. It involves visiting the site where the product is used and observing the usage in action. It can reveal interesting insights on environmental circumstances affecting the usage of the product, and supplementary tools and work-arounds used along with the product.

For more information, refer to:

Courage, C & Baxter, B. 2005. Understanding Your Users: A Practical Guide to User Requirements Methods, Tools, and Techniques.

11.1.2 *Contextual inquiry*

The contextual inquiry research technique combines observation with interview-style question and response. Participants get to explain their actions or "think aloud" as they work through a task or activity.

For more information refer to:

Holtzblatt, K.Wendell, J.B. & Wood. S. 2004. Rapid Contextual Design: A how-to guide to key techniques for user-centered design.

11.2 SURVEYS / QUESTIONNAIRES

Surveys or questionnaires are useful to gather information on the profile of the user, his or her job responsibilities and opinion of the current version of product (if available) or similar product (if this is a new release). It is easy to collect both quantitative and qualitative information using surveys. Surveys may be online or face-to-face. Online surveys may be conducted using tools such as SurveyMonkey[46].

---

46. http://www.surveymonkey.com/

Face-to-face surveys may be conducted in combination with observational techniques such as site visits or in a usability lab.

It is important to know how to ask the right questions the right way to get quality input for design. This means not asking leading or confusing questions. For more information refer to:

Alreck, P.L & Seatle, R.B. 1995. The survey research Handbook

Salant, P. & Dillman, D 1994. How to Conduct your Own Survey

11.3 FOCUS GROUPS

A focus group is a qualitative research technique where a group of individuals are asked their opinions, perceptions, beliefs, attitudes or practices regarding a product, service or concept. It is important to pay attention to group dynamics when conducting a focus group since the loudest voice may dominate the conversation and drown out other opinions.

For more information refer to:

David W. Stewart, Prem N. Shamdasan Focus Groups: Theory and Practice

11.4 INTERVIEWS

Interviews are a "guided conversation where one person seeks information from the other." An interview may be conducted in conjunction with other requirements-gathering activity such as a site visit, or as a solo activity.

There are various types of interview you can choose from based on your project needs and constraints. Interviews may be conducted remotely (via the phone), or face to face. A structured interview is one where the list of questions is prepared in advance and the researcher tries to solicit answers from all participants. A nondirected interview is one where the interviewer primarlity listens to the subject and provides minimal input or direction.

For more information refer to:

Weiss, R.S. 1995. Learning from Strangers: The Art and Method of Qualitative Interview Studies

11.5 DIARY STUDIES

A diary study involves asking the test participants to record and report their experiences related to a particular subject over a period of time. Depending on the type of study, participants may use paper diaries, emails, twitter or a combination. Such studies can be flexible and easy to execute. They are particularly appropriate for understanding mobile device usage since it allows the user to provide their input on-the-go.

Like most research methods, diary studies need to be well designed and have a focus to be effective. A poorly designed study may yield a lot of data that may be difficult to sift through to create meaning.

For more information refer to:

Sharon, T. 2012. It's Our Research: Getting Stakeholder Buy-in for User Experience Research Projects

11.6 BRAINSTORMING

Brainstorming is a tool for creative problem solving, wherein a group of people come together to contribute ideas spontaneously. It is particularly useful when you want to break out of stale, established patterns of thinking, so that you can develop new ways of looking at things. When a interdisciplinary product team brainstorms to come to a common vision of the solution, it helps get buy-in for the chosen solution.

For more information refer to:

Kelley, T. 2001. The Art of Innovation: Lessons in Creativity from IDEO, America's Leading Design Firm.

11.7 GAMESTORMING

Gamestorming, as the name suggests, refers to the use of games for brainstorming. The term Innovation Games also refers to this technique. Presenting the problem in a game format suspends some of the normal protocols of life and frees the participants to think creatively to solve problems. For example, if the goal is to prioritize a list of features in a product, gamestorming may involve giving each participants a limited set of resources and allowing them to buy / bet on features to see which ones come out on top.

For more information refer to:

Gray, D. 2010. Gamestorming: A Playbook for Innovators, Rulebreakers, and Changemakers.

11.8 WEB ANALYTICS

Web analytics refers to gathering and analyzing usage data to gain insights into consumer actions and attitudes. Tools such as Google Web Analytics and Omniture have made it possible for companies to adopt a real data driven approach to understanding usage patterns to optimize the experience for the user. In the case of gamification, it is very useful to know the impact on player behavior to adjust and optimize the strategy as needed.

For more information refer to:

Kaushik, A. 2009. Web Analytics 2.0: The Art of Online Accountability and Science of Customer Centricity.

11.9 PLAYTESTING

A playtest is a type of usability testing, in which a game designer tests a new game for bugs and design flaws before release. The target player types are recruited via various methods, and are given the game to play. The designers observe the participants and study usage statistics to collect qualitative and quantitative data on the product. They then iterate to make the product better. This practice is beneficial to gamification as well.

For more information refer to:

Schell, J. 2008. The Art of Game Design: A book of lenses.

11.10 A/B TESTING

A/B testing is an experimental approach to user experience design. It presents two versions of a website (Option A and Option B) to the user, and analyzes users' behavior. Typically, it tries to track the effect of the differences of the two options against a desired goal. For example, if a website is trying to increase click through rate, they may present a version to one set of online users, and a different version to another. They could analyze if these differences have any impact on the metric they care about.

For more information refer to:

McFarland,C. 2012. Experiment!: Website conversion rate optimization with A/B and multivariate testing.

11.11 OTHER RESEARCH METHODS

When designing enterprise products, it is helpful to know the domain via online research. Researching competiors is an important part of the initial 360- degree research for any product. Analyst and market research reports usually provide good insight into industry trends and business practices.

Professional communities like LinkedIn offer groups for specialized categories of users. Browsing such communities can provide a way to build empathy for your target users by getting a glimpse of their view of the world.

11.12 CUSTOMER CO-INNOVATION PARTNERSHIPS

Enterprise software companies creating standard applications for business practices need intimate knowledge of work practices in their customer's organization. For established business processes, this information is obtained through recruiting target users that fit the user profile into a user research project. When it comes to innovative business processes, however, the normal recruiting methods fall short due to:

▶ Need for Customer Trust: True breakthrough innovation such as gamification in the enterprise software context, requires an in-depth understanding of the domain, business process, and employee motivations. Customers are hesitant to share these details with a standard software maker since this information could be shared with their competitors.

▶ Limited supply of target participants: The type of player may not yet widely exist in the population and therefore the availability is limited. For example, if we are building a solution to leverage social media in call centers, this business practice is still emerging and therefore the available pool of recruits is limited. This increases the time needed for recruiting.

▶ Innovation takes iteration: When creating a transformational product, the team needs to be prepared to try a few different options.

This means even more rapid recruiting to facilitate rapid iteration and feedback cycles. This, along with the limited supply of participants to begin with makes research a challenge for innovative products, and gamification is no exception.

Customer Co-innovation Partnerships addresses these issues by:

▶ Upfront agreement building trust: By its very nature, this is a partnership agreement between the customers and software makers to innovate. Non-Disclosure agreements are signed by both parties, to assure each other that the information gathered will be used to inform the design activities, and any sharing beyond this will be strictly restricted. Similarly, the customers will have access to early designs and prototypes, and such artifacts may not be distributed. This builds trust on both sides, and enables sharing of insights.

▶ Target player identification: As part of the upfront co-innovation partnership, the customer can help identify the right people in the organization who can provide input. Since they know their employees better than the external software vendor does, it reduces recruitment effort and increases the quality of the interviews and feedback.

▶ Iterative validations: Once the correct target participants have been identified, reaching out to them for periodic validation and input is usually not an issue. Studies may be shorter since the researcher need not pack all the research questions into one study.

▶ Innovative research methods: Once the trust is established via the co-innovation agreement, the team may explore innovative research methods such as Gamestorming to generate many ideas for innovation in partnership with the customer.

There are benefits for the customer too:

- ▶ Early influence: Customers who participate in co-innovation have early influence over the product. They are shaping the product to best fit their business process vision.

- ▶ Early adoption: These co-innovation partners get the right to be early adopters before their competitors. This head-start advantage could translate into an opportunity to increase market share away from their competition.

- ▶ Cost savings: Since the product was designed to meet their needs, the implementation, training, and adoption costs are reduced for the customers participating in co-innovation.

We recommend having three to six co-innovation customers.Fewer than three runs the risk of becoming a customer development project for these specific customers and more than six is hard to manage due to administrative logistics.

YOUR NOTES AND THOUGHTS ON CHAPTER 11

Record your notes and thoughts on this chapter. If you want to share these thoughts with others online, go to the bottom of the page at: http://www.interaction-design.org/books/gamification_at_work/chapter_11_curated_list_of_research_techniques.html

NOTES:

_____

_____

_____

_____

_____

_____

_____

_____

Acknowledgements

Janaki Kumar

This book could not have been written without the support of my family. My three daughters—Sahana, Sithara and Sonali—you inspire me every day, and you teach me more than I can ever hope to teach you. My husband Pravin—thank you for being my rock. You reviewed every word I wrote and were my sounding board. Thanks to the Kumar clan for being such good sports about me spending weekends and evenings in my home office writing this book.

Thanks to my mentors—Don Norman, an inspiration, who has always encouraged me to write, and on whom I count on for candid and thoughtful feedback. Thanks to Michael Arent who reviewed every chapter with care and gave me great input.

Thanks to Tim Thianthai, who created all the illustrations in this book. Tim, you are awesome! Thanks to Julien Altieri who suggested the pacman player persona. Thanks to Sahana Kumar for the early sketches and brainstorming.

Thanks to my co-author Mario for being a fun guy to work with. This book represents our many years of collaboration.

Mario Herger

I thank Pacman, Angry Birds, and all other games for having given me so much joy during all the years.

Not least for the reason that my wife and I get some well-deserved rest from parenting, while our son is playing them.

COPYRIGHT TERMS

Open Access

We believe in Open Access and the **democratization of knowledge**. Unfortunately, world class educational materials are normally hidden behind payment systems or in expensive textbooks. If you want this to change, you should **help us out!** Kind thoughts are **not** enough - you need to act!

Copyright Terms

We do **NOT** use copyright as a restrictive instrument, but as an instrument **to protect the author against misuse while encouraging redistribution and use of his/her work**. As such, these copyright terms are designed for the author and the reader, not the publisher and the profit.

Except as otherwise noted, this work is copyright of Janaki Mythily **Kumar** and Mario **Herger** and The Interaction Design Foundation (Chr. Molbechs Vej 4, DK-8000 Aarhus C, Denmark) and is licensed under the following terms:

   i.   The Creative Commons Attribution-NoDerivs Licence

   ii.   The Interaction Design Foundation Addendum to the Creative Commons licence

...with the exception of materials described in...:

   iii.   "Exceptions"

i. Creative Commons Attribution-NoDerivs 3.0 Unported

The Creative Commons Attribution-NoDerivs 3.0 Unported License

1. Definitions

   a.   **"Adaptation"** means a work based upon the Work, or upon the Work and other pre-existing works, such as a translation, adaptation, derivative work, arrangement of music or other alterations of a literary or artistic work, or phonogram or performance and includes cinematographic adaptations or any other form in which the Work may be recast, transformed, or adapted including in any form recognizably derived from the original, except that a work that constitutes a Collection will not be considered an Adaptation for the purpose of this License. For the avoidance of doubt, where the Work is a musical work, performance or phonogram, the synchronization of the Work in timed-relation with a moving image ("synching") will be considered an Adaptation for the purpose of this License.

b. **"Collection"** means a collection of literary or artistic works, such as encyclopedias and anthologies, or performances, phonograms or broadcasts, or other works or subject matter other than works listed in Section 1(f) below, which, by reason of the selection and arrangement of their contents, constitute intellectual creations, in which the Work is included in its entirety in unmodified form along with one or more other contributions, each constituting separate and independent works in themselves, which together are assembled into a collective whole. A work that constitutes a Collection will not be considered an Adaptation (as defined above) for the purposes of this License.

c. **"Distribute"** means to make available to the public the original and copies of the Work through sale or other transfer of ownership.

d. **"Licensor"** means the individual, individuals, entity or entities that offer(s) the Work under the terms of this License.

e. **"Original Author"** means, in the case of a literary or artistic work, the individual, individuals, entity or entities who created the Work or if no individual or entity can be identified, the publisher; and in addition (i) in the case of a performance the actors, singers, musicians, dancers, and other persons who act, sing, deliver, declaim, play in, interpret or otherwise perform literary or artistic works or expressions of folklore; (ii) in the case of a phonogram the producer being the person or legal entity who first fixes the sounds of a performance or other sounds; and, (iii) in the case of broadcasts, the organization that transmits the broadcast.

f. **"Work"** means the literary and/or artistic work offered under the terms of this License including without limitation any production in the literary, scientific and artistic domain, whatever may be the mode or form of its expression including digital form, such as a book, pamphlet and other writing; a lecture, address, sermon or other work of the same nature; a dramatic or dramatico-musical work; a choreographic work or entertainment in dumb show; a musical composition with or without words; a cinematographic work to which are assimilated works expressed by a process analogous to cinematography; a work of drawing, painting, architecture, sculpture, engraving or lithography; a photographic work to which are assimilated works expressed by a process analogous to photography; a work of applied art; an illustration, map, plan, sketch or three-dimensional work relative to geography, topography, architecture or science; a performance; a broadcast; a phonogram; a compilation of data to the extent it is protected as a copyrightable work; or a work performed by a variety or circus performer to the extent it is not otherwise considered a literary or artistic work.

g. **"You"** means an individual or entity exercising rights under this License who has not previously violated the terms of this License with respect to the Work, or who has received express permission from the Licensor to exercise rights under this License despite a previous violation.

h. **"Publicly Perform"** means to perform public recitations of the Work and to communicate to the public those public recitations, by any means or process, including by wire or wireless means or public digital performances; to make available to the public Works in such a way that members of the public may access these Works from a place and at a place individually chosen by them; to perform the Work to the public by any means or process and the communication to the public of the performances of the Work, including by public digital performance; to broadcast and rebroadcast the Work by any means including signs, sounds or images.

i. **"Reproduce"** means to make copies of the Work by any means including without limitation by sound or visual recordings and the right of fixation and reproducing fixations of the Work, including storage of a protected performance or phonogram in digital form or other electronic medium.

2. Fair Dealing Rights. Nothing in this License is intended to reduce, limit, or restrict any uses free from copyright or rights arising from limitations or exceptions that are provided for in connection with the copyright protection under copyright law or other applicable laws.

3. License Grant. Subject to the terms and conditions of this License, Licensor hereby grants You a worldwide, royalty-free, non-exclusive, perpetual (for the duration of the applicable copyright) license to exercise the rights in the Work as stated below:

a. to Reproduce the Work, to incorporate the Work into one or more Collections, and to Reproduce the Work as incorporated in the Collections; and,

b. to Distribute and Publicly Perform the Work including as incorporated in Collections.

c. For the avoidance of doubt:

   i. **Non-waivable Compulsory License Schemes**. In those jurisdictions in which the right to collect royalties through any statutory or compulsory licensing scheme cannot be waived, the Licensor reserves the exclusive right to collect such royalties for any exercise by You of the rights granted under this License;

   ii. **Waivable Compulsory License Schemes**. In those jurisdictions in which the right to collect royalties through any statutory or compulsory licensing scheme can be waived, the

Licensor waives the exclusive right to collect such royalties for any exercise by You of the rights granted under this License; and,

iii.   **Voluntary License Schemes**. The Licensor waives the right to collect royalties, whether individually or, in the event that the Licensor is a member of a collecting society that administers voluntary licensing schemes, via that society, from any exercise by You of the rights granted under this License.

The above rights may be exercised in all media and formats whether now known or hereafter devised. The above rights include the right to make such modifications as are technically necessary to exercise the rights in other media and formats, but otherwise you have no rights to make Adaptations. Subject to Section 8(f), all rights not expressly granted by Licensor are hereby reserved.

4. Restrictions. The license granted in Section 3 above is expressly made subject to and limited by the following restrictions:

a.   You may Distribute or Publicly Perform the Work only under the terms of this License. You must include a copy of, or the Uniform Resource Identifier (URI) for, this License with every copy of the Work You Distribute or Publicly Perform. You may not offer or impose any terms on the Work that restrict the terms of this License or the ability of the recipient of the Work to exercise the rights granted to that recipient under the terms of the License. You may not sublicense the Work. You must keep intact all notices that refer to this License and to the disclaimer of warranties with every copy of the Work You Distribute or Publicly Perform. When You Distribute or Publicly Perform the Work, You may not impose any effective technological measures on the Work that restrict the ability of a recipient of the Work from You to exercise the rights granted to that recipient under the terms of the License. This Section 4(a) applies to the Work as incorporated in a Collection, but this does not require the Collection apart from the Work itself to be made subject to the terms of this License. If You create a Collection, upon notice from any Licensor You must, to the extent practicable, remove from the Collection any credit as required by Section 4(b), as requested.

b.   If You Distribute, or Publicly Perform the Work or Collections, You must, unless a request has been made pursuant to Section 4(a), keep intact all copyright notices for the Work and provide, reasonable to the medium or means You are utilizing: (i) the name of the Original Author (or pseudonym, if applicable) if supplied, and/or if the Original Author and/or Licensor designate another party or parties (e.g., a sponsor institute, publishing entity, journal) for attribution ("Attribution Parties") in Licensor's copyright notice, terms of service or by other reasonable means, the name of such party or parties; (ii) the title of the Work if supplied; (iii) to the extent reasonably practicable, the URI, if any, that Licensor specifies to be associated with the Work, unless such URI does not refer to the copyright notice or licensing information for the Work. The credit required by this Section 4(b) may be implemented in any reasonable manner; provided, however, that in the case of a Collection, at a minimum such credit will appear, if a credit for all contributing authors of the Collection appears, then as part of these credits and in a manner at least as prominent as the credits for the other contributing authors. For the avoidance of doubt, You may only use the credit required by this Section for the purpose of attribution in the manner set out above and, by exercising Your rights under this License, You may not implicitly or explicitly assert or imply any connection with, sponsorship or endorsement by the Original Author, Licensor and/or Attribution Parties, as appropriate, of You or Your use of the Work, without the separate, express prior written permission of the Original Author, Licensor and/or Attribution Parties.

c.   Except as otherwise agreed in writing by the Licensor or as may be otherwise permitted by applicable law, if You Reproduce, Distribute or Publicly Perform the Work either by itself or as part of any Collections, You must not distort, mutilate, modify or take other derogatory action in relation to the Work which would be prejudicial to the Original Author's honor or reputation.

5. Representations, Warranties and Disclaimer

UNLESS OTHERWISE MUTUALLY AGREED TO BY THE PARTIES IN WRITING, LICENSOR OFFERS THE WORK AS-IS AND MAKES NO REPRESENTATIONS OR WARRANTIES OF ANY KIND CONCERNING THE WORK, EXPRESS, IMPLIED, STATUTORY OR OTHERWISE, INCLUDING, WITHOUT LIMITATION, WARRANTIES OF TITLE, MERCHANTIBILITY, FITNESS FOR A PARTICULAR PURPOSE, NONINFRINGEMENT, OR THE ABSENCE OF LATENT OR OTHER DEFECTS, ACCURACY, OR THE PRESENCE OF ABSENCE OF ERRORS, WHETHER OR NOT DISCOVERABLE. SOME JURISDICTIONS DO NOT ALLOW THE EXCLUSION OF IMPLIED WARRANTIES, SO SUCH EXCLUSION MAY NOT APPLY TO YOU.

6. Limitation on Liability. EXCEPT TO THE EXTENT REQUIRED BY APPLICABLE LAW, IN NO EVENT WILL LICENSOR BE LIABLE TO YOU ON ANY LEGAL THEORY FOR ANY SPECIAL, INCIDENTAL, CONSEQUENTIAL, PUNITIVE OR EXEMPLARY DAMAGES ARISING OUT OF THIS LICENSE OR THE USE OF THE WORK, EVEN IF LICENSOR HAS BEEN ADVISED OF THE POSSIBILITY OF SUCH DAMAGES.

7. Termination

a.   This License and the rights granted hereunder will terminate automatically upon any breach by You of the terms of this License. Individuals or entities who have received Collections from You under this License, however, will not have their licenses terminated provided such individuals or entities remain in full compliance with those licenses. Sections 1, 2, 5, 6, 7, and 8 will survive any termination of this License.

b.   Subject to the above terms and conditions, the license granted here is perpetual (for the duration of the applicable copyright in the Work). Notwithstanding the above, Licensor reserves the right to release the Work under different license terms or to stop distributing the Work at any time; provided, however that any such election will not serve to withdraw this License (or any other license that has been, or is required to be, granted under the terms of this License), and this License will continue in full force and effect unless terminated as stated above.

8. Miscellaneous

a. Each time You Distribute or Publicly Perform the Work or a Collection, the Licensor offers to the recipient a license to the Work on the same terms and conditions as the license granted to You under this License.

b. If any provision of this License is invalid or unenforceable under applicable law, it shall not affect the validity or enforceability of the remainder of the terms of this License, and without further action by the parties to this agreement, such provision shall be reformed to the minimum extent necessary to make such provision valid and enforceable.

c. No term or provision of this License shall be deemed waived and no breach consented to unless such waiver or consent shall be in writing and signed by the party to be charged with such waiver or consent.

d. This License constitutes the entire agreement between the parties with respect to the Work licensed here. There are no understandings, agreements or representations with respect to the Work not specified here. Licensor shall not be bound by any additional provisions that may appear in any communication from You. This License may not be modified without the mutual written agreement of the Licensor and You.

e. The rights granted under, and the subject matter referenced, in this License were drafted utilizing the terminology of the Berne Convention for the Protection of Literary and Artistic Works (as amended on September 28, 1979), the Rome Convention of 1961, the WIPO Copyright Treaty of 1996, the WIPO Performances and Phonograms Treaty of 1996 and the Universal Copyright Convention (as revised on July 24, 1971). These rights and subject matter take effect in the relevant jurisdiction in which the License terms are sought to be enforced according to the corresponding provisions of the implementation of those treaty provisions in the applicable national law. If the standard suite of rights granted under applicable copyright law includes additional rights not granted under this License, such additional rights are deemed to be included in the License; this License is not intended to restrict the license of any rights under applicable law.

ii. The Interaction Design Foundation Addendum to the Creative Commons licence

The Interaction Design Foundation Addendum to the Creative Commmons licence is a placeholder for additions to the Creative Commons licence, which are deemed necessary to include in consideration of Danish law and the operation of this site and The Interaction Design Foundation.

1. Attribution

If this work is used under the licencing conditions set forth here, attribution must be clearly given, i.e. the author's name, the title and URL of this work/publication/web page must clearly appear. The attribution must be given in a manner appropriate to the medium in which it is given: For example, electronic copies must include a clickable URL, which does not use the nofollow attribute value.

2. Updates

Internet technology, publishing technology, and the applicable laws, rules, and regulations change frequently. Accordingly, The Interaction Design Foundation reserves the unilateral right to update, modify, change and alter its Site Terms and Conditions as well as Copyright Terms at any time. All such updates, modifications, changes and alterations are binding on all users and browsers of Interaction-Design.org, readers of electronic and non-eletronic versions of the publications produced by The Interaction Design Foundation. Such updates will be posted on Interaction-Design.org.

iii. Exceptions

Exceptions

Many materials published by The Interaction Design Foundation - both in print and electronically - may contain materials where the copyright is owned by a third party, e.g. another publisher. In this case, the copyright status depends on the third party, i.e. the copyright owner, and may for example be "all rights reserved - used with permission". When this is the case, we clearly label the content. For images, we both write the specific copyright label (including attribution) underneath the caption in both electronic and print copies as well as include the copyright label (including attribution) inside the image file (i.e. the full-resolution version) in metadata types like EXIF, IPTC, and XMP. We only include and label content with the following copyright terms:

1. Pd:

    Public Domain (information that is common property and contains no original authorship)

    Legal Code (full licence text): http://en.wikipedia.org/wiki/Public_domain

2. CompositeWorkWithMultipleCopyrightTerms:

    Work that is derived from or composed of multiple works with varying copyright terms and/or copyright holders

3. FairUse:

    Copyrighted materials that meet the legal criteria for Fair Use when used by the Interaction Design FoundationThe most common cases of Fair Use are: 1) Cover art: Cover art from various items, for identification only in the context of critical commentary of that item (not for identification without critical commentary). 2) Team and corporate logos: For identification. 3) Other promotional material: Posters, programs, billboards, ads: For critical commentary. 4) Film and television screen shots: For critical commentary and discussion of the cinema and television. 5) Screenshots from software products: For critical commentary. 6) Paintings and other works of visual art: For critical commentary, including images illustrative of a particular technique or school. 7) Images with iconic status or historical importance: As subjects of commentary. 8) Images that are themselves subject of commentary.

Legal Code (full licence text): http://en.wikipedia.org/wiki/Fair_use

4. AllRightsReservedUsedWithoutPermission:

All Rights Reserved. Non-free, copyrighted materials used without permission. The materials are used without permission of the copyright holder because the materials meet the legal criteria for Fair Use and/or because The Interaction Design Foundation has not been able to contact the copyright holder. The most common cases of Fair Use are: 1) Cover art: Cover art from various items, for identification only in the context of critical commentary of that item (not for identification without critical commentary). 2) Team and corporate logos: For identification. 3) Other promotional material: Posters, programs, billboards, ads: For critical commentary. 4) Film and television screen shots: For critical commentary and discussion of the cinema and television. 5) Screenshots from software products: For critical commentary. 6) Paintings and other works of visual art: For critical commentary, including images illustrative of a particular technique or school. 7) Images with iconic status or historical importance: As subjects of commentary. 8) Images that are themselves subject of commentary.

5. AllRightsReserved:

All Rights Reserved. Materials used with permission. Permission to use has been granted exclusively to The Interaction Design Foundation and/or the author of the given work/chapter, in which the copyrighted material is used. This permission constitutes a non-transferable license and, as such, only applies to The Interaction Design Foundation. Therefore, no part of this material may be reproduced, stored in a retrieval system or transmitted in any form or by any means, electronic, recording or otherwise without prior written permission of the copyright holder.

6. CC-Att-1:

Creative Commons Attribution 1.0 Unported
Legal Code (full licence text): http://creativecommons.org/licenses/by/1.0/

7. CC-Att-3:

Creative Commons Attribution 3.0 Unported
Legal Code (full licence text): http://creativecommons.org/licenses/by/3.0/

8. CC-Att-2:

    Creative Commons Attribution 2.0 Unported

    Legal Code (full licence text): http://creativecommons.org/licenses/by/2.0/

9. CC-Att:

    Creative Commons Attribution 3.0 Unported

    Legal Code (full licence text): http://creativecommons.org/licenses/by/3.0/

10. CC-Att-ND-3:

    Creative Commons Attribution-NoDerivs 3.0 Unported

    Legal Code (full licence text): http://creativecommons.org/licenses/by-nd/3.0/

11. CC-Att-ND-2:

    Creative Commons Attribution-NoDerivs 2.0 Unported

    Legal Code (full licence text): http://creativecommons.org/licenses/by-nd/2.0/

12. CC-Att-ND-1:

    Creative Commons Attribution-NoDerivs 1.0 Unported

    Legal Code (full licence text): http://creativecommons.org/licenses/by-nd/1.0/

13. CC-Att-ND:

    Creative Commons Attribution-NoDerivs 3.0 Unported

    Legal Code (full licence text): http://creativecommons.org/licenses/by-nd/3.0/

14. CC-Att-SA-1:

    Creative Commons Attribution-ShareAlike 1.0 Unported

    Legal Code (full licence text): http://creativecommons.org/licenses/by-sa/1.0/

15. CC-Att-SA-3:

    Creative Commons Attribution-ShareAlike 3.0

    Legal Code (full licence text): http://creativecommons.org/licenses/by-sa/3.0/

16. CC-Att-SA-2:

    Creative Commons Attribution-ShareAlike 2.0 Unported

    Legal Code (full licence text): http://creativecommons.org/licenses/by-sa/2.0/

17. CC-Att-SA:

    Creative Commons Attribution-ShareAlike 3.0 Unported

    Legal Code (full licence text): http://creativecommons.org/licenses/by-sa/3.0/

18. Unknown:

    Copyright status unknown

19. Trademarks and logos:

    All trademarks, logos, service marks, collective marks, design rights, personality rights or similar rights that are mentioned, used or cited by The Interaction Design Foundation and its authors are the property of their respective owners. The use of any trademark in our materials does not vest in the author or The Interaction Design Foundation any trademark ownership rights in such trademarks, nor does the use of such trademarks imply any affiliation with or endorsement of The Interaction Design Foundation and its authors by such owners. As such The Interaction Design Foundation can not grant any rights to use any otherwise protected materials. Your use of any such or similar incorporeal property is at your own risk. Words which we have reason to believe constitute trademarks may or may not have been labelled as such. However, neither the presence nor absence of such labels should be regarded as affecting the legal status of any trademarks.

While most material produced by The Interaction Design Foundation is free to use under its respective license as outlined above, some materials may be subject to additional legal restrictions when they are used in particular circumstances or in particular ways. These limitations may arise from laws related to trademarks, patents, personality rights, political censorship, or any of many other legal causes which are entirely independent from the copyright status of the work. For example, if you use a public domain image (i.e. uncopyrighted) of an apple to sell computers, you will violate the trademark rights of Apple Computer, Inc.

In addition, content linked from a page/chapter/book (in the online versions) is not covered by one of our licenses unless specifically noted. For example, pages may link to videos or slide decks that are not covered. The design of Interaction-Design.org (graphics, html, client-side scripts, etc.) is copyright of Mads Soegaard.

CPSIA information can be obtained
at www.ICGtesting.com
Printed in the USA
LVOW02s0145270317
528515LV00002B/6/P